THE RUSSO-JAPANESE WAR

SPECIAL CAMPAIGN SERIES. No. 10

THE RUSSO-JAPANESE WAR

A SKETCH

FIRST PERIOD—THE CONCENTRATION

By

CAPTAIN F. R. SEDGWICK
ROYAL FIELD ARTILLERY

WITH MAPS AND PLANS

The Naval & Military Press Ltd

Published by

The Naval & Military Press Ltd
Unit 5 Riverside, Brambleside
Bellbrook Industrial Estate
Uckfield, East Sussex
TN22 1QQ England

Tel: +44 (0)1825 749494

www.naval-military-press.com
www.nmarchive.com

Cover illustration:
Picture of Our Valorous Military Repulsing the Russian Cossack Cavalry on the Bank of the Yalu River
by Watanabe Nobukazu

In reprinting in facsimile from the original, any imperfections are inevitably reproduced and the quality may fall short of modern type and cartographic standards.

Print and page size has been increased over the original publications to accommodate the oversized maps.

PREFACE

At present the data necessary to enable a detailed account of the late war in the Far East to be written is not accessible, and will not be so until the Russian and Japanese General Staffs have produced full accounts of the operations.

In compiling the sketch of the war comprised in the present volume the following works have been chiefly relied on:—

1. Russo-Japanese War, Part I. By the General Staff.
2. Russo-Japanese War, Part II. By Historical Section of the Committee of Imperial Defence.
3. Reports of British Officers attached to Russian and Japanese forces.
4. Kriegsgeschichtliche Einzelschriften, Parts 37, 38, 39, 40, 41, 42. By German Great General Staff.
5. A Staff Officer's Scrap Book. By General Sir Ian Hamilton, K.C.B., D.S.O.
6. Achtzehn Monate mit Russlands Heeren in der Mandschurei. By Freiherr von Tettau.

In cases where there seems a conflict of testimony, or where I have quoted the words of an authority, a reference is made in a footnote.

The following is a complete list of authorities thus quoted.

Name of Work.	Author.	Referred to as
The Russo-Japanese War, Part I.	The General Staff	G. S. i.
,, ,, ,, Part II.	Historical Section of Committee of Imperial Defence	G. S. ii.
A Staff Officer's Scrap Book	Sir Ian Hamilton	I. H.
Reports of British Officers	Edited by the General Staff	B. O. R.
The Russo-Japanese War, Official Japanese Reports	Translated by M. Kinai	O. R.
Hamley's Operation of War, 6th Edition, Part VI. chap. i.	Colonel Kiggell	Kiggell.
Notes on Artillery in Manchuria	Major Geddes	Geddes.
La Guerre Russo-Japonaise	Meunier	Meunier.
,, ,,	E. Bujac	Bujac.
Der Russisch-Japanische Krieg	Löffler	Löffler.
,, ,, ,,	Immanuel	Immanuel.
Kriegsgeschichtliche Einzelschriften	German Great General Staff	K. E.
The Russo-Japanese Conflict	Dr Asakawa	Asakawa.
The Truth about Port Arthur	Nojine (translated)	Nojine.
Achtzehn Monate mit Russlands Heeren in der Mandschurei	Freiherr von Tettau	F. v. T.
Conferences sur la Guerre Russo-Japonaise	Lectures at the Russian Staff College (translated into French)	Conferences.
Revue de d'Artillerie	... ...	R. d'A.
Revue Militaire des Armées étrangères	... ...	R. M. d'A. E.
Journal des Sciences Militaires		J. S. M.
Revue Militaire Générale		R. M. G.
Streffleurs Militärische Zeitschrift		S. M. Z.
Journal of Royal United Service Institution		R. U. S. I. J.
Royal Artillery Institution Proceedings		R. A. I. P.
Journal of the United Service Institution of India		U. S. I. of India.

In studying this campaign, not the least of the many difficulties is, that every place has at least three names given to it—Chinese, Japanese and Russian. These names were variously rendered in English, French and German. I have endeavoured throughout to adopt the spelling used in the publications issued under the authority of the General Staff. While this book was actually in the press, and the maps had already been completed, Part II. Russo-Japanese War, by the Historical Section of the Committee of Imperial Defence, was published. There are, therefore, one or two very slight and, I hope, unimportant discrepancies between the spelling in the maps published with this book and that of the beautiful maps published with the official account.

Finally, I would ask my reader's indulgence to one who is but a beginner should my account be obscure in places, or difficult to follow.

F. R. SEDGWICK,
Capt. R.F.A.

Exeter, 26th December 1908.

CONTENTS

CHAPTER	PAGE
I. Introduction	1
II. The First Operations	33
III. Events in May	61
IV. Events in June	82
V. Events in July	119
VI. A Summary	171

LIST OF MAPS

I. THE THEATRE OF WAR
II. THE LIAOTUNG PENINSULA. SITUATION END OF APRIL
III. BATTLE OF THE YALU
IV. BATTLE OF NANSHAN
V. THE LIAOTUNG PENINSULA. SITUATION END OF MAY
VI. BATTLE OF TELISSU
VII. THE FENSHUILING PASS
VIII. THE LIAOTUNG PENINSULA. SITUATION END OF JUNE
IX. BATTLE OF TASHICHIAO
X. BATTLE OF HSIMUCHENG
XI. BATTLE ON THE EAST FRONT, 31ST JULY
XII. THE LIAOTUNG PENINSULA SITUATION AFTER THE ACTION OF THE 31ST JULY

In pocket at end of book.

THE RUSSO-JAPANESE WAR

CHAPTER I

Political Events leading up to the War—The general Causes—The Strength of Russia—The Strength of Japan—The Theatre of War in general—Railways—Rivers—Korea—Manchuria—Sea Communication—Situation in the Theatre of War in February 1904—A Russian Division—A Japanese Division—General strategical Outlook

EVER since Russia became a united empire, she has steadily striven to free for herself a road to **Russia in Asia** the open sea. In Europe her way has been blocked by Turkey, and, more recently, by a barrier of small Slav states; but in Siberia, into which country her first settlers penetrated some 300 years ago, she has succeeded in reaching the ocean. In 1860 she obtained by pressure on the Chinese government, the cession of the eastern coast of Manchuria from the Amur to the Korean frontier, and with it the important harbour of Vladivostok. Still even that gave her no port ice-free for all the year round, for Vladivostok is closed for nearly four months in the twelve. The seaway from Vladivostok to the Pacific Ocean leads through the straits of La Pérouse, between the islands of Sakhalin and Yezo; in 1875 Russia forced Japan to exchange Sakhalin for the Kuriles Islands.

In order to consolidate her position in the Far East, it was decided to build a railway across Siberia to Vladivostok. Many years elapsed before the intention was put into practice, but in 1896 the line had been constructed as far eastwards as Strietensk, with a gap at Lake Baikal, on which steamers plied in summer and sledges in winter; from Vladivostok a line stretched west to Khabarovsk.

In this year a Russian company obtained a concession to construct a railway through Manchuria from Chita via Harbin, to connect the two portions of the Siberian railway.

For centuries the empire of Korea, which juts out from the mainland of Asia towards Japan, has

Korea   been, although a vassal of China, a bone of contention between China and Japan. The misgovernment and unsettlement of Korea was chronic, and in 1875 an outrage on a Japanese steamer by Koreans caused Japan to intervene in Korea, ignoring Chinese suzerainty. In 1882 further outbreaks occurred in Korea; in 1885 Japan and China concluded the "Tientsin Convention," agreeing to withdraw from Korea, but if either found it necessary to again send troops there, to give the other due notice.

In 1894 serious outbreaks in Korea obliged the Chinese government to send troops there, whereupon Japan occupied Fusan and Chemulpo. After the rebellion had been quelled, Japan suggested that certain reforms should be inaugurated in Korean administration; and when China refused to admit the right of Japan to interfere, war broke out between these two great Mongol states.

The Chino-Japanese War

A diary of the war is of interest as showing a similarity with the war of 1904.

 25th July 1894—A Chinese transport sunk.

 30th July—Disembarkation of Japanese troops at Fusan and Gensan in Korea.

 August—The Japanese concentrated the 5th Division at Séoul.

 16th September—Naval battle off the Yalu.

 25th October—Engagement and passage of Yalu river.

 24th October—A second Japanese army landed in the Kwantung peninsula and captured Chinchou.

 31st October—Fenghuangcheng occupied.

Port Arthur was taken by storm and the Yalu army advanced on Haicheng. A part of the second army also advanced on that point, and the two armies united about Newchuang and Yinkou, attacked, and defeated the Chinese on the Liao river.

The treaty which closed this war was signed at Shimonoseki on the 10th April 1895, and by it Japan received Formosa, the Pescadores, the Liaotung peninsula, and a war indemnity of £25,000,000, while China recognised the independence of Korea. At this point, however, Russia, France, and Germany intervened, and forced Japan to accept a further £5,000,000 instead of the Liaotung peninsula. In 1897 Germany forced China to lease the Kiaochau territory to her, **Kiaochau** and England followed suit by obtaining the important harbour of Wei-hai-wei. These proceedings induced Russia to "lease" the Kwantung peninsula and France to "lease" Kuangchouwan. The construction of a railway **The Chinese** from Harbin to Dalny and Port Arthur **Eastern** was begun in 1899. To guard this **Railway** line Russian troops were posted at various points in Manchuria.

In 1900 a rebellion known as the Boxer rebellion broke out in China; allied troops from all the **The Boxer** Powers pushed on to, and occupied, **Rebellion** Pekin, while Russia occupied the Manchurian railway line still more securely.

In 1902 Great Britain and Japan concluded a defensive alliance which secured either of the two parties "fair play" if war became inevitable in the East, for the two Powers contracted that, in the event of either becoming involved in war with a third Power in defence of its interests in the Far East, if a further Power or Powers intervened, mutual assistance should be rendered.

The Anglo-Japanese Alliance

In the same year Russia undertook to evacuate Manchuria; but in October the evacuation had not commenced, and certain demands were made by Russia on China.

Russia and China

In 1896 and 1898 Russia and Japan had signed agreements recognising the independence of Korea, but in 1902 Russian troops began to enter Korea, to guard valuable Russian timber concessions on the Yalu and Tumen rivers.

Russia and Korea

These facts and the terms of the Russian demands on China, gave the impression that Russia did not intend either to evacuate Manchuria or to respect the integrity of Korea, and representations on the subject were made by Japan to Russia in 1903. In August, 1903, a draft treaty was presented at St Petersburg, which included the demand of Japan to the exclusive right to give advice and assistance to Korea. Many drafts of treaties were exchanged,

Russia and Japan

and on 13th January 1904, Japan finally stated that she would regard Manchuria as outside her sphere of influence if Russia would give a similar undertaking with regard to Korea. No reply being received, on 6th February the Japanese Minister at St Petersburg withdrew from the Russian capital.

Such is a brief outline of the political events leading to the war. The more fundamental issues, however, as in many another international crisis, seem to be oftener understood than expressed, and hence understood only vaguely; yet it may be said that they constitute the very forces which have, with irresistible certainty, brought the belligerents into collision. For Japan the issues appear to be partly political, but mainly economical.[1] To this we may fairly add that the issues were not only political and economical, but also moral. The economical issues arose from two causes: first the enormous growth in the population in Japan—34,000,000 in 1875, 46,305,000 on 31st December 1903;[2] secondly the quite amazing growth in Japanese foreign trade, and particularly that with Manchuria and Korea. In the latter country practically the whole, and in the former by far

Further Causes of the War

Economical Cause of the War

[1] Asakawa, p. 1.   [2] Official figures.

the larger part, of the ever-increasing volume of foreign trade was in Japanese hands.

No nation, not even America, could compete with Japan in these markets, and therefore "from Japan's point of view Korea and China must be left open freely to the economic enterprise of herself and others alike."[1] Russia's aim was diametrically opposed to this, and as Mr Asakawa says, "Russia's interests were intelligible as are Japan's, but unfortunately their desires were antagonistic to one another, so that a conflict between an open and an exclusion policy was rendered inevitable."

The moral causes of the war are deeper, but form perhaps the most serious of all the issues involved in this great struggle. The onward march of the European across the continent of Asia had met with effete nations and governments whose opposition had proved of the weakest. India is in the hands of the British, "the Turkoman horses are harnessed to the guns of the Russian Czar," Pekin had been occupied, and the Chinese, a commercial race, appeared unable to prevent the dismemberment of their territories. Thus to Japan, as indeed to all Asia, it seemed that it was reserved for the race of sailors and warriors that dwelt in the

Moral Causes of the War

[1] Asakawa, p. 52.

furthest islands that fringe Asia, to stem the tide of invasion, or else to finally confess that the White is the superior of the Yellow and the Brown. Such a sentiment is more easily felt than expressed; but there is no doubt that it existed, and helped wonderfully to make it seem light to the people of Japan to bear the weight and cost of the long war, and the preparation for it.

Once again the war has proved that a people whose training teaches them to place their country's honour first and personal comfort second, who esteems it an honour to be called to undergo the hardships of a military training, is capable of nobler efforts, and is, in short, a better race than one whose first thought is for peace to collect riches, the only use of which is to purchase personal comfort. There is no possible doubt as to which of the two great Mongol races, the Chinese or the Japanese, stands highest in the estimation of the world to-day; and history will confirm the verdict. That position has been won by the sword, and must be kept by the sword. Is it not possible that there may be some lesson in this for the British people?

The empire of Russia, which is singularly homogeneous, covers an area of over 8,250,000

Russia square miles, and had an estimated population in 1904 of close on 140,000,000 souls, of whom fully 120,000,000 are Russians. The ordinary revenue in 1904 amounted to £208,000,000, and her total debt to about £750,000,000.[1]

Financial There was no reason to doubt that Russia could borrow any imaginable amount of money necessary to enable her to carry on a war almost indefinitely.

Army Her army at the commencement of the war consisted of:[2]

Active army with reserves	3,500,000
Cossacks	345,000
Militia	684,000
Caucasian native troops	12,000

a grand total of 4,541,000 men.

The army is classified as follows:—Field troops, depôt troops, fortress troops, local troops, national militia.

The standing army consisted of:

1. Twenty-nine army corps (two in Turkestan, two in East Siberia)
2. Various cavalry divisions and brigades, rifle brigades, and other troops.

The composition of army corps varies, and the numbers of those taking part in the war will be from time to time stated; each consisted of

[1] *Whitaker's Almanack.* [2] G. S., p. 27.

two divisions and corps troops. The whole male population is liable to serve for eighteen years in the active army, and for five years in the militia. The Cossacks and Finns serve under special terms.

The men who form the rank and file of the Russian army are almost all il-literate peasants, of fine physique and heroic endurance. The Russian soldier has proved beyond dispute that defeat after defeat does not destroy his moral; when well led he is a most formidable enemy, but, as he lacks education and intelligence, resource and initiative cannot be expected of him. The officers are, like the men, brave and enduring, but are drawn from very varying social classes. The staff was highly trained.

The Rank and File of the Russian Army

The Officers

The Cossacks and cavalry were trained alike for dismounted and mounted action, but their musketry instruction was incomplete, and the men of the Cossack corps were wholly illiterate, and worthless at reconnaissance.[1] The artillery was formed in brigades of two, three, or four batteries of eight guns. It was in process of re-armament with a quick-firing gun at the outbreak of the war. Indirect laying had been little practised.[2]

Organisation and Armament

[1] F. v. T., i. p. 66.
[2] J. de S. M., 11th series, vol. v. p. 257. Article by Colonel Novikoff.

The infantry was trained to believe that shock tactics in close order are the methods to employ on the battlefield. In peace and war the soldier marched and fought with bayonet fixed. "By exalting out of all reason moral forces at the expense of technical science, the mere shock at the expense of capacity to manœuvre, Dragomiroff, disciple of Suvaroff, the apostle of the bayonet, had had no difficulty in persuading his compatriots that the rifle is only a handle for his favourite weapon, and that nothing could withstand the *élan* of the Russian soldier. What then was the good of working!"[1]

Undoubtedly this statement has much truth, but it omits the fact that the soul of Dragomiroff's teaching was that the "spirit of the troops" is the most important thing in war. It was the fault of the Russian officers that Dragomiroff's teaching was twisted to mean that labour at instruction in fire action and battle tactics were unnecessary for the Russian soldier.[2]

Political Condition of Russia
It should not be forgotten that the political condition of Russia was one of extreme unrest, and that the feeling of the people, and therefore of the soldiery, was not altogether in sympathy with the war.

"Besides the poor war training of the rank and

---

[1] Meunier, p. 55. [2] F. v. T., i. p. 8.

file, the incapacity of the lower and the higher grades of Russian leaders to work alone or to assume the initiative was particularly noticeable."[1]

Russian Officers

All observers noticed the slackness of discipline among the officers, and the general carelessness and laziness. The system of promotion, by which officers of the guards got their promotion to command of regiments before ordinary line officers could get their companies, did not tend to increase any ardour for work. Promotion was by favour pure and simple.

During the war constant bickering amongst the generals had a most disintegrating effect on the sum of the operations. The picture of affairs in Port Arthur as drawn by Nojine, though probably highly coloured, reveals how serious this want of co-operation was. Red tape was rampant. There is a story of Nojine's that 300 men were sent north from Port Arthur after the Yalu in a great hurry. They wore "part worn," not "new," tunics, according to regulation. They were returned to be fitted with new tunics.

The Russian system of supply is, ordinarily, to provide a regimental commander with money to purchase supplies for his men. In Manchuria this was not always possible, and the "intendance" procured enor-

Transport and Supplies

[1] K. E., 39, 40, p. 35.

mous quantities of provisions. The system was that the quartermaster-general informs the chief intendant officer where troops are going to, and this officer works out what rations will be required, and at what points. The intendance officer then requisitions on the transport department to convey the rations.

Beyond the railway the transport consists of the regimental transport, divisional supply columns, and special (auxiliary) transport columns. It seems that in the regimental and divisional transport eight days' biscuits and six days' groats were carried. The transport vehicles consisted of four-wheeled waggons and two-wheeled carts. These latter were the ordinary vehicle in Manchuria. Pack transport was also employed, but not largely. The special (auxiliary) transport columns were non-existent at the commencement of the war, and were only slowly formed. The want of transport was destined to hamper severely the Russian movements.

Each company was provided with a two-wheeled field kitchen; these were most successful.

The medical arrangements of the Russian army were almost entirely taken over by the Red Cross

Medical Society. This society supplemented the military medical corps, which has only a peace establishment, and no reserve. Thus in

August, 1904, between Harbin and Liaoyang there were forty-three Red Cross hospitals of 200 beds, besides the Red Cross ambulance section with the fighting troops in front of Liaoyang.

Naval forces Russia's naval strength was divided into her Baltic and Pacific fleets.

In the Pacific she had:

> 7 battleships
> 4 armoured cruisers
> 7 protected cruisers
> 2 guardships
> 2 torpedo gunboats
> 26 destroyers
> 18 torpedo boats
> 4 mining boats

and a few other gunboats, etc.

In the Baltic:

> 8 battleships
> 3 second-class battleships
> 3 armoured cruisers
> 6 protected cruisers

besides other vessels.

The Japanese forces Japan is a collection of islands covering an area of 162,655 square miles, and with a population of about 47,000,000. The annual revenue of 1903-1904 was £25,500,000, and the debt £57,500,000.[1]

[1] *Whitaker's Almanack.*

Army

At the outbreak of war the army of Japan consisted approximately of:[1]

Active and Reserve (Yobi) Army	380,000
2nd Reserve (Kobi)	200,000
Conscript Reserve (Hoju)	50,000
Trained men of the National Army	220,000

a total of 850,000 trained men.

Besides these were:

Untrained Conscript Reserve	250,000
Untrained men available for service in the National Army	4,000,000

The standing army was organised into:

> 13 divisions
> 2 cavalry brigades
> 2 artillery brigades
> Certain guards and garrison troops

The reserve (Kobi) army consisted of thirteen brigades, generally, but not always, mixed brigades, one of which was affiliated to each active division. On the outbreak of war depôt units were formed by infantry, cavalry, and artillery regiments to keep their own regiments and affiliated Kobi units up to strength.

The system of conscription had been introduced into Japan in 1871, and superseded the earlier feudal system. Every Japanese who is physically fit, is liable to service in the army or navy, but only the number required is

The Personnel

[1] G. S., p. 20.

taken by lot, a portion going to the active army and thence to the reserve army, and a portion to the conscript reserve. The officers were a most highly educated and trained body of men, and the staff, formed on the German model, most remarkably efficient.

The Japanese soldier, nearly a foot shorter on the average than his Russian opponent, was none the less a most formidable fighter. Of splendid constitution, great endurance, and very cleanly habits, he proved well able to stand the hardships of a campaign; and the spirit of patriotism and self-sacrifice that animated all ranks has been descanted on so often as to be by now too well known to need recounting.

Organisation and Armament

The cavalry was armed with sword and carbine, and trained for shock action, but also to fight on foot; the men, though picked, were poor horsemen, and the horses were overweighted.[1] The artillery was organised in battalions of three batteries, and trained to work as such. Particular stress was laid on the importance of concealment. They were armed with a 2.95-inch gun of 13.23 lbs., with a range of 5000 yards. The mountain and field artillery guns were the same calibre. There were also some batteries of 4.72-inch howitzers.

[1] G. S., p. 22.

The infantry was armed with a .256-inch magazine rifle, and was trained to believe that the great object of the attack was to obtain fire superiority, and that "the aim of every man must be to press forward regardless of loss, and that any wavering or lack of dash would lead to increased casualties and diminish the chances of success."

The infantry took about 200 rounds into action, but this was increased by a peculiarity of their **Infantry Equipment** equipment. This consisted of a blue cloth bag about six feet long and nine inches wide, and divided in the middle. Rations could be carried in one part, and an extra 200 rounds in the other. When an action was impending, the knapsacks were discarded and the men went into action with the holdall worn *en bandoulière* across the right shoulder. Thus equipped they were able to support a lengthy engagement.

The Japanese arrangements for supply and transport were as thorough as the rest of their army organisation. Each division had nucleus **Supply and Transport** troops for transport services organised into a "train" battalion. The men for this service were trained for only three months, but were recruited in the same way as for the combatant services. The ammunition supply train was under the artillery; doctors and medical personnel were attached as required to the ambulance train. Pack transport (chiefly donkeys) was used, but a man-handled light cart proved the most suitable method. The ordinary horse transport cart was two-wheeled, and proved too weakly constructed for the work. For auxiliary transport on the lines of communication Chinese carts and Korean coolies were employed, étapen posts being established and supplies pushed up from post to post. It seems that six days' rations were carried with the troops, two days' in the regimental transport, four days' in the divisional train.[1]

Financial

Japan, being a poor country, would require to borrow very largely to carry on a great war. The "hard-headed business man," as the papers love to call him, is singularly susceptible to influences which are often more sentimental than real. One single Japanese failure would probably cause him to shut up his purse. The Japanese had therefore to fight with one eye upon the exchanges of London and New York.

Japanese Navy

The Japanese fleet was, of course, concentrated (but for two cruisers) in the Far East, and consisted of:

      7 battleships
      6 first-class cruisers
      12 second-class cruisers
      13 third-class cruisers

[1] Bujac, p. 93.

14 gunboats
19 destroyers
70 torpedo boats

The map shows Japan stretching over 1000 miles along the eastern coast of Asia. It was obvious **The Theatre** that the war must be fought out in the **of War** waters of the Yellow Sea and Sea of Japan, and in Korea, Manchuria, and the eastern provinces of Siberia.

Russia was connected with Eastern Siberia and Port Arthur by a single line of railway 5000 miles long from Moscow to Harbin. At Harbin **Railways** the line divides, passing south to Port Arthur 550 miles, and east to Vladivostok 300 miles. At Tashichiao, 360 miles south of Harbin, a branch runs to Yinkou, while from Newchuang there is a line to Pekin. From Hsinmintun, a few miles west of Mukden, a line runs south to Pekin, connecting with the Newchuang-Pekin line.

In Korea there was a line twenty miles long from Chemulpo to Séoul, and another under construction from Fusan to Séoul (forty miles completed).

The rivers were not, with the exception of the Amur and its tributaries, of much value. The Yalu is navigable in summer for junks **Rivers** for some fifty miles, the Tumen is hardly navigable at all. The Liao from Yinkou is navigable as far as Newchuang for small steamers, and for junks in times of high water to beyond Mukden.[1]

Both the Yalu and Liao are frozen in winter. The Amur, however, is navigable up to Strietensk during the summer months, and its tributaries, the Ussuri and Nonni, are also navigable for a long way.

Korea

The peninsula of Korea, some 500 miles long and 150 broad, juts out from the continent of Asia towards Japan, from which it is separated by the Korean straits. Opposite its southern extremity is the celebrated Inland Sea of Japan, and right in the centre of the straits is the fortified island of Tsushima.

Korea's southern and western coasts afford many good harbours, but on the east there is only one, that of Gensan. The country is mountainous, the population scanty and mainly engaged in agriculture; but, for a considerable force, supplies are not procurable locally. There is not a road worthy of the name in the country, and in wet weather the tracks are well-nigh impassable. The southern limit of ice is roughly Chinampo on the west coast and Gensan on the east. Gensan is, however, difficult in winter.

[1] J. of U. S. I. of India. Article by Captain Archdale, R. H. A., vol. xxxiv.

Manchuria

Manchuria may be divided roughly into two districts. Firstly the valleys of the great rivers, the Liao and the Amur and its tributaries. These valleys form rich alluvial plains, wonderfully fertile, and, for an almost purely agricultural community, densely populated, covered with small towns, villages, and isolated homesteads. The houses are substantially built of clay. This district supplied immense quantities of grain, forage, fowls, and pigs for the Russian armies. Secondly the mountains, which so far as Southern Manchuria are concerned, lie west of the railway line which skirts them. These mountains consist of a confused jumble of hills, shutting in narrow valleys which are themselves broken into by spurs which, running down into the valleys, enclose steep ravines. The mountains in the Liaotung peninsula are bare of trees; north of it, however, they are forest-clad. In the mountainous district the population is scanty, and confined to the valleys.

The main chain of the mountains of Eastern Manchuria is known as the Shanaling. In the Liaotung the range is locally called the Chienshan or Thousand Peaks, and is divided into the Fenshuiling and Hsiungyaoshan ranges, while further to the north is the Taling ridge.[1]

[1] G. S. ii., 29.

Roads There are no roads in the country; but important tracks, called Mandarin roads, run, one from Port Arthur via Fuchou and Liaoyang to Mukden, and another from Korea by Antung and Fenghuangcheng to Liaoyang and thence to Pekin. This latter road crosses the main ridge by a series of passes, of which the most important is the Motienling; the new road, however, crosses by a pass just north of this latter. From Takushan one road runs to Hsiuyen and thence via the Fenshuiling (or Daling) Pass to Hsimucheng and Haicheng; another passes by the Chipanling Pass to Kaiping. There is a road along the coast from Antung to Chinchou. From Shuitien on the Yalu a road runs to Aiyangcheng, connecting there with one from Fenghuangcheng, and thence by Saimachi, Chiaotou, and Penhsihu to Mukden. It will be seen that this road was of some strategical importance, for a force placed at Fenghuangcheng would threaten at the same time Liaoyang, Mukden, and the railway south of Liaoyang by the roads through Hsiuyen.

Climate The climate is temperate in summer, but extremely cold in winter. In the rainy season, July and August, the low-lying country becomes a great swamp, and the torrents often make a road temporarily quite impassable.

Mongolia The province of Mongolia is extremely rich in cattle and ponies, and contributed enormous numbers of both to the Russian "intendance."

The position of Japan placed communication by sea between Vladivostok and Port Arthur at the
Communication by Sea mercy of the Japanese fleet, and the communications between Japan and Fusan could hardly be seriously disturbed unless Russia gained complete control of the sea.

The coast line of Southern Manchuria is a difficult one for the operation of landing troops.

The limit of ice is, roughly, Gensan on the east, Chemulpo on the west. The ports of the Kwantung peninsula are always ice-free.

The brief remarks above and a study of the map will enable us to form a fair idea of the respective
Comments situations before the war. On the one side we find a very great and powerful nation with almost limitless resources, but handicapped by material difficulties in transporting her men to a distant frontier, and by the moral disadvantages that the hearts of her people were not in sympathy with the war, and by the fact that her troops were not sufficiently educated and trained for modern fighting. On the other side we find a nation smaller, but with its power concentrated, close to hand, and possessing the moral advantages which Russia lacked. So remarkably did this affect Sir Ian Hamilton that he actually had

the courage to prophesy the event before the war.[1]

Distribution in Feb. 1904

It is now necessary to examine how each side had its forces distributed at the time of the outbreak of hostilities.

The Russian fleet of seven battleships, six cruisers, thirteen torpedo boats, etc., was at Port Arthur; four first-class cruisers and some torpedo boats were at Vladivostok; and the *Variag*, a second-class cruiser, with the gunboat *Koreetz*, were at Chemulpo.

Naval Forces

The Japanese fleet was concentrated in the Inland Sea.

Army

The Russian forces east of Lake Baikal consisted, so far as can be judged, of:[1]

```
Field troops:
    Infantry (96 battalions)       .   .   92,000
    Cavalry (35 squadrons)         .   .    5100
    Artillery (25 batteries, 196 guns) .    6400
    Engineers (13 companies)       .   .    2700
            Total       .   .   .   .   106,200
    Fortress troops    .   .   .   .     7700
    Railway troops     .   .   .   .    11,450
    Frontier guards, 55 companies,
        55 squadrons, 6 batteries (48 guns) 23,450
            Total combatant strength   148,800
```

[1] I. H., p. 4. [1] G. S., p. 32.

It is believed, however, that at the commencement of the campaign the strength of a battalion was only about 700, and of a squadron about 100, and thus the total field troops would amount only to some 80,000 men. It must be remembered, too, that these troops were scattered over an immense area, and had still to garrison the fortresses and guard the railway.

The distribution of the field troops was probably much as follows:—

1. Vladivostok and Ussuri District:
    48 battalions
    12 squadrons
    4 companies engineers
    112 guns
2. Kwantung Peninsula and Southern Manchuria:
    30 battalions
    12 squadrons
    8 companies engineers
    40 guns
3. On or near railway south of Harbin:
    8 battalions
    11 squadrons
    12 guns

Thus the actual force at the end of April available for active operations, could hardly have exceeded 60,000 bayonets, 3500 sabres, and 164 guns.[1]

The field troops in the Far East, except two infantry brigades, were organised in brigades of

[1] G. S., p. 34.

rifle regiments of two battalions each, and regiments of artillery of three batteries. To increase these to a war footing it had been decided to increase the rifle regiments to three battalions and artillery brigades to four batteries. These reinforcements were to come from Russia.

Strength of a Russian Division
This seems a fitting point to give the general strength of a Russian and a Japanese division. Every Russian division consisted of:

> 2 brigades of infantry of 2 regiments each
> 1 brigade of artillery

In a Siberian Rifle Division

> Each rifle regiment had 3 battalions
> The brigade of artillery, 4 batteries (of 8 guns)

In an Infantry Division

> Each regiment had 4 battalions
> The brigade of artillery, 6 or 8 batteries (of 8 guns)

Thus the strength was:

> Rifle divisions: 12 battalions
>   32 guns
> Infantry divisions: 16 battalions
>   48 or 64 guns

Cossack Brigade
A Cossack brigade consisted of two regiments of six squadrons, and generally a 6-gun horse artillery battery.

Engineers
Engineer battalions were part of an army corps.

Japanese Division

A Japanese division consisted of:

Cavalry.—1 regiment (of 3 squadrons)
Infantry.—2 brigades of 2 regiments (of 3 battalions)
Artillery.—1 regiment, 6 batteries (of 6 guns)
Engineers.—1 battalion (of 3 companies)

Total
- 3 squadrons
- 12 battalions
- 36 guns
- 3 companies engineers

Six divisions had field artillery.

Six divisions had mountain artillery.

One division had three batteries field, three batteries mountain.

Kobi Brigade

A Kobi brigade consisted of

2 regiments of 2 battalions
Total, 4 battalions

Mixed Kobi Brigade

A "mixed" Kobi brigade was an independent unit, and had as combatant troops:

6 battalions
3 batteries
1 company engineers

Cavalry Brigade

A cavalry brigade consisted of

2 regiments of 4 squadrons
Total, 8 squadrons

An Artillery Brigade

An artillery brigade consisted of

3 regiments of 6 batteries
Total, 108 guns

Allowing for the fact that the Russian strengths were not complete, it may be taken that a Russian infantry division was 12,000 strong, with forty-eight to sixty-four guns; a Siberian rifle division, with which in the earlier part of the war we are chiefly concerned, 8500, with thirty-two guns; a Japanese division was at least 12,000, with thirty-six guns.

Comparison of Russian and Japanese Divisions

The Russian forces on land and sea were commanded by the viceroy Admiral Alexieff, a man of sixty-one years of age. He had served in the navy, but held many shore appointments. He had commanded the fleet in eastern waters in 1897 and 1898, had charge of the Kwantung Peninsula 1899-1903. In August, 1903, he had been nominated viceroy. He was a representative of the Russian forward party in East Asia.

Admiral Alexieff

In Vladivostok the troops were commanded by General Linevitch, a veteran of every war since his enlistment. He was sixty-six years old, and had risen from the ranks.

General Linevitch

Admiral Starck

The fleet was commanded by Admiral Starck, an undistinguished personality.

The chief of the General Staff of Japan was Marshal Oyama, a man of sixty-two years of age. He had commanded the army in China for a short time, and had a great reputation for solidity and capability.

Marshal Oyama

Admiral Togo The fleet was commanded by Admiral Togo, who had served in every grade and seen service in the China War.

In considering the general outlook it may be permissible to quote Colonel Kiggell's clear exposition of the situation. He says: "Assuming success of the Japanese on the sea, it was necessary to have plans ready for the next move. What should be the first objective on land? What would be the best line of operation? Must the army remain idle while the situation was developing, or could it do something meanwhile?"[1] And he answers these questions thus: "On land or on sea the enemy's fighting forces must be the first objective. When his forces are divided *that which is most immediately dangerous should usually be first dealt with.*" The most immediately dangerous portion of the Russian force was obviously the Port Arthur squadron, which so long as it was "a fleet in being" was a standing menace to the communication of the Japanese army with its base in Japan; "a fact which led to a peculiarly complicated strategical problem in which a Russian fleet became the objective of a Japanese army." Port Arthur was

[1] Kiggell, p. 361.

also to the Japanese a political and moral factor of the highest importance. Its position gave it its political importance; its moral importance lay in the fact that it had once already been a Japanese possession, and Russia was the active cause of its having been given up. In its recovery, as it seemed to the Japanese, lay the road to the recovery of Japanese honour.

The Russians were bound to concentrate on the railway. To attack them Japan must advance either from Vladivostok on Harbin, or from Port Arthur on Harbin. The first line would threaten the communications of troops south of Harbin, the second of troops east of Harbin. The first line would necessitate a landing on a barren coast, ice-bound till April, and the siege of a powerful fortress. True the line of the Amur might be used in summer, but that was far off. The other line was obviously better. There are good ports on the Liaotung peninsula, the navy would secure the left flank of the advance as far as Yinkou, and enable sudsidiary bases to be formed. An army operating from Korea could unite with one from the south about Liaoyang, whereas to unite with one from Vladivostok would require a most arduous march. Lastly, in either case Port Arthur must be attacked by land as well as sea.

It should be reiterated that Korea must be occupied by Japan, this being the chief prize of the war.

It is obvious then that the first operations of the war must take place at sea. While these operations were taking place, Japan would occupy Korea, entering the country either from Fusan or, if possible, from Chemulpo. To prevent this Russian troops might push down either from Mukden or from Vladivostok. From either direction, however, they must pass most difficult country, and it was quite certain that such an advance could only be made in comparatively small numbers.

Having secured the command of the sea, which it seemed certain Japan would secure, even if not completely yet in a great measure, and having secured her position in Korea, Japan would attack Port Arthur, and having landed troops for the siege would push a covering force northwards.

On the Russian side the first object must be to mobilise all existing troops in Siberia, place Port Arthur and Vladivostok in a position of defence, bring up some of her immense resources from European Russia, and send out her fleet from European waters to the Far East.

It is believed that the original Russian plan contemplated a concentration of troops about Harbin to the number of six army corps and three cavalry divisions as a field army.[1] This operation would

[1] B. O. R., i. p. 68.

take six months. It was believed that plenty of time would be available, and the opinion was freely expressed that the further the Japanese penetrated into Manchuria the better.[1] The position of Port Arthur and the fleet there would, it was hoped, make the Japanese transport of troops difficult.

[1] F. v. T., i. pp. 8, 9, 29, 70, etc.

CHAPTER II

The first Operations—The Japanese Landing at Chemulpo—Naval Engagement off Chemulpo—Naval Engagement off Port Arthur—Further Naval Operations—The Advance through Korea—The Position at the end of April—Russians—Japanese—The Battle of the Yalu—The Action at Hamatang—Losses—Comments

Chemulpo

On the evening of the 4th February 1904 the Japanese government decided to despatch a squadron to Chemulpo and another to Port Arthur; but to avoid precipitating matters at Chemulpo, where a Russian transport ship lay with troops on board, orders to mobilise the army were withheld. It was important to anticipate Russia in Korea, for in the first place the western ports would afford secure bases for Togo's fleet, and in the second place the southern ports would be denied to the Russians.[1]

At 6 P.M. on the 5th February four battalions of the 12th Division, at peace strength, were ordered to embark and occupy Séoul. By 2 A.M. on the 6th they were embarking, and at 2 P.M. the convoy,

[1] G. S., p. 42.

escorted by Admiral Uriu with a cruiser division of seven cruisers and twelve torpedo boats, left Sasebo. On the 7th the cable between Port Arthur and Chemulpo was cut, and a Japanese cruiser at Chemulpo put to sea. At 5.15 P.M. on the 8th the convoy appeared off Chemulpo, having met the *Koreetz* and exchanged shots; by 3 A.M. on the 9th the four battalions were on shore and two were moved up to occupy Seoul. At 6 A.M. on the 9th the Japanese cruisers left harbour, and Uriu demanded the surrender of the *Variag* and *Koreetz*. These boats gallantly went out to meet their fate. The *Variag* was badly damaged and returned with the *Koreetz* to port, when the crews blew up the vessels and went on board neutrals.

Meanwhile at 6 P.M. on the 8th the fleet under Admiral Togo had concentrated at Round Island, sixty miles from Port Arthur. Three divisions of destroyers proceeded at once to Port Arthur and attacked the Russian fleet at anchor in the roadstead. On the 9th Togo attacked the Russians with the main fleet, and the result of the two engagements was that seven of the Russian battleships and cruisers were severely damaged, and the fleet was obliged to take refuge in the harbour. On the 9th the four Russian cruisers at Vladivostok put to sea, but accomplished little.

Port Arthur

As this work is entirely concerned with the military operations, and only with those of the two fleets in so far as they affected the operations on land, it may be as well to summarise here the whole of the operations at sea during the early part of the war. On the 14th February a naval attack on Port Arthur was made and a Russian cruiser was damaged. On the 16th two cruisers purchased in Europe arrived in Japan. On the 17th Admiral Makharoff, a man of about fifty-five, with a very high professional reputation, succeeded Starck in command of the Russian fleet at Port Arthur, and infused a new spirit of energy into it. On 24th February an attempt was made to block the entrance to Port Arthur harbour by sinking ships in the fairway. This attempt was renewed on the 27th March, on the 27th April, and on the 1st May; but the attempts were all unsuccessful, though the last was supposed at first to have succeeded. On the 21st and 22nd March and on the 15th April the fleet bombarded Port Arthur. On the 13th April the Russian fleet issued from Port Arthur, but was driven back, and a battleship with Makharoff on board was sunk by a mine. On the 15th May a Japanese cruiser was sunk in a collision, and another struck a mine. On the 15th June the Vladivostok cruiser squadron sunk two Japanese transports conveying troops of the 6th Division.

On the 23rd June the Russian fleet again issued

from Port Arthur and again was driven back; and on the 10th August the fleet issued out again, but was dispersed and destroyed. On the 14th August Kamimura caught and attacked the Vladivostok cruiser squadron and sank the *Rurik*. In sum, the Japanese navy was universally successful, defeated and destroyed or blockaded the Russian fleets, and preserved inviolable the seaway from Japan to the ports of Southern Manchuria and Korea; finally it established a close blockade of the Kwantung peninsula to assist the siege of Port Arthur.

Reverting to the military operations, the landing at Chemulpo showed how carefully every detail had been prepared for. The transports towed or carried sampans (large flat-bottomed boats), which carry thirty to forty men, or five to ten horses. They also carried piers all ready cut, and fitted so that they could be put together in a few hours. As each body of troops landed it was passed on at once, without confusion. With the supplies were landed at the same time the coolies and carts to remove them. The absence of noise and confusion was marked by all who witnessed the operation.

The Disembarkation at Chemulpo

On the 6th February the guard, 2nd, and 12th Divisions, were ordered to mobilise. By the 14th the 12th Division had completed mobilisation and embarked at Nagasaki in six

Japanese Mobilisation

groups. By the 21st the whole division had disembarked at Chemulpo. Two regiments (4th Division) were sent to Séoul and Fusan; Masampo and Gensan were occupied and garrisoned by Japanese troops.

Comment

"Thanks to sea power and the prompt despatch of troops, Chemulpo had been secured as a landing-place and the occupation of Séoul effected without opposition. These successes had saved the 12th Division the long march from Fusan to the capital, and for the benefit of the troops that soon would follow from Japan an experiment somewhat similar might be repeated further north."[1]

Pingyang occupied

At present, however, Chinampo was still icebound, but on the 21st February a Japanese detachment had occupied Pingyang, and posts were established between that town and Séoul. On the 23rd the cavalry of the 12th Division reached Pingyang, and was followed on the 25th by the leading infantry. By the 18th March the 12th Division had cleared Pingyang,

Anju occupied

and on the 10th Anju was occupied by cavalry supported by a force of four battalions,[2] which occupied the line of the Chechen river.

Meanwhile on the 10th March a landing was

[1] G. S., p. 45.   [2] G. S., p. 45.

effected at Chinampo, and an advanced force of the guard and 2nd Division, consisting of the divisional cavalry (six squadrons), an infantry regiment, two battalions of engineers, and two telegraph companies,[1] landed there on the 13th. A portion of this force marched at once for Anju, and by the 18th the force there had reached a strength of eight squadrons, five battalions, one battalion engineers.[2] The remainder of the guard and 2nd Division completed their disembarkation by the 29th.

Disembarkation of Troops at Chinampo

The engineers had been at work on the roads, but in the middle of March, when the thaw set in, they became well-nigh impassable. As, however, the Russian force on the south bank of the Yalu was reported to consist only of some 1500 to 2000 cavalry, General Kuroki, the commander of the 1st Army, as the force of three divisions in Korea was now called, decided to push forward, and ordered the Chechen and Taing rivers to be bridged; a covering force of seven squadrons, two batteries, and five battalions was sent forward from Anju.

Arrangements for an Advance

The supply question was the chief difficulty. Reconnaissance had shown that the only practicable road was that along the coast; the bulk of the army, therefore, followed this road, while

[1] G. S., p. 46. [2] G. S., p. 46.

a right-flank detachment was sent along a road farther inland.

On the 28th March the guard cavalry and a small force of infantry engaged 600 Russian cavalry near Tiessu and occupied that place. On the 31st supplies reached Anju by boat, and thus on the 1st April the advanced troops were able to move. These consisted of:

>5 squadrons
>2 batteries mountain artillery
>3 battalions
>1 company engineers

Supplies were landed at points along the coast, five depôts being formed, of which the most important was Rikaho;[1] and by 7th April enough stores had been collected for the main army to advance.

On the 4th April the advanced troops reached Wiju and Yongampo, the 12th Division being in support south of Tiessu. The flank guard (one squadron, two batteries mountain artillery, three battalions) held Yongpyon, and was to march on Siojo.[2] The main army advanced as follows: on the 4th April the 12th Division in two columns at a day's interval, then at two days' interval the guards, also in two columns at a day's interval,

The 1st Army advances

[1] G. S., p. 48.   [2] G. S., p. 48.

last at three days' interval the 2nd Division in two columns at a day's interval.

On the 8th and 9th there was a terrible storm which destroyed bridges and delayed the march; however, the supplies at Rikaho were not injured. On 8th April the advance guard entered Wiju, and on the 21st the concentration south of Wiju of the whole army was completed, with lines of communication to Rikaho, Boto, and Quiempo. On the 20th the flank guard had reached Chiangsyong.

The movement had been slow, but when the difficulties are considered not only does it appear that **Comment** this was inevitable, but that the march was really a rapid one.[1]

Turning now to the Russian movements, Admiral Alexieff, the viceroy and commander-**Russian** in-chief in the Far East, had done **Movements** his best to remedy the unfortunate state of unpreparedness in which the forces were. Still the work was slow, and it was not before the end of April that the reorganisation, mobilisation, and concentration of the troops east of Lake Baikal were complete.[2] In the course of this concentration the peace arrangements were absolutely ignored, and as a result the staffs did not know the troops, nor in many cases even the regimental officers their men. For the concentra-

[1] G. S., p. 49.   [2] F. v. T., i. 64.

tion the railway was almost entirely used, and was fully occupied. Thus the forwarding of reinforcements from Russia was not possible.

To command the troops in Southern Manchuria under Alexieff, General Kuropatkin, a soldier of **General Kuropatkin** the greatest ability, who as a young man had been chief of the staff to Skobeleff outside Plevna, was despatched from St Petersburg, where he was the War Minister. He had the full confidence of the Czar, the nation, and the army, and was an indefatigable worker.[1] He was fifty-six years old.

The first step taken in the mobilisation had been to send a supply of rolling stock across Lake Baikal, which was at that time frozen solid; sixty-five locomotives and about 2400 trucks[2] were thus conveyed across. More sidings were constructed, and work pushed forward on the new railway round the lake.

Steps in the Mobilisation It has been said that on mobilisation the East Siberian Rifle Brigades were to be converted to divisions by sending from Russia an extra battalion to each regiment and a fourth battery to each division. A new division had also just been formed, the 9th East Siberian Rifle Division. The line was, therefore, taken up during January, February, March, and April in conveying to their places of mobilisation and moving thence

[1] F. v. T., i. 63.   [2] R. M., vol. lxiii. 375.

to their places of concentration stores, supplies and ammunition, and the following troops:—

1. The 9th E. S. R. Division [1]
2. 3rd Sapper Battalion
3. Reservists for Brigades of 31st and 35th Infantry Divisions at Vladivostok
4. 3rd Battalions and 4th Batteries [2]
5. Reservists of the Rifle Divisions and of the I. Siberian Infantry Division
6. 6 regiments of Cossacks
7. Advanced troops of IV. Siberian Corps

It gives some idea of the time required, that to mobilise the IV. Siberian Corps, which is localised west of Lake Baikal, and consists of the 2nd and 3rd Siberian Infantry Divisions, it would take forty-one days.

The capacity of the trans-Siberian line has been much discussed. The *Novoe Vremya*, a Russian paper, published an official statement which is of interest. During February and March three to four trains per diem were run each way, in April five trains, in June seven trains, in August eight trains, and so on until the maximum of thirteen trains a day each way were run. The trains were long, thirty-two carriages; excellent arrangements for food, etc.,

Capacity of trans-Siberian Railway

[1] K. E., 39, 48, p. 49.
[2] Required to complete the E. S. R. brigades to the footing of divisions. *Vide* preceding paragraph.

were made, and Freiherr von Tettau testifies that the horses stood the journey perfectly. The circum-Baikal line was opened on the 25th September. Towards the end of April the Russian forces began to assume a fairly definite shape.

Troops available at end of April

In the Kwantung peninsula was General Stoessel, with General Smirnoff, a distinguished engineer, as fortress commandant. To defend Port Arthur he had:

> 4th and 7th E. S. R. Divisions
> 5th E. S. R. Regiment (2nd E. S. R. Division)
> 1 sotnia of Cossacks
> Fortress troops
> Total field troops $\begin{cases} 1 \text{ squadron} \\ 27 \text{ battalions} \\ 56 \text{ guns} \end{cases}$

In or near Vladivostok General Linevitch had under his command:

> 8th E. S. R. Division
> 2nd E. S. R. Division (less 1 regiment)
> One and a half regiments of Cossacks
> Fortress and railway troops
> Total field troops $\begin{cases} 9 \text{ squadrons} \\ 21 \text{ battalions} \\ 56 \text{ guns} \end{cases}$

The Manchurian Field Army under the direct command of General Kuropatkin:

East detachment (or advanced guard on the Yalu), General Zassulich:
 3rd E. S. R. Division
 6th E. S. R. Division (less 1 regiment)[1]
 1 mountain battery
 Half 2nd Sapper Battalion
 One machine gun detachment

General Mischenko's trans-Baikal Cossack Brigade:
 1 horse artillery battery
 Argansk and Ussuri Cossack Regiments

Colonel Madritoff's detachment:
 2 squadrons
 2 detachments mounted scouts[2]

Total field troops { 24 squadrons / 21 battalions / 62 guns / Half battalion engineers

I. Siberian Army Corps (General Stakelberg) posted about Yinkou and Taschichiao:
 1st and 9th E. S. R. Divisions
 Primorsk Dragoon Regiment
 1 regiment of mounted frontier (or railway) guards
 1 horse artillery battery

II. Siberian Army Corps (General Vassilieff) posted about Liaoyang and Haicheng:
 5th E. S. R. Division
 2nd Brigade 31st Infantry Division (X. Corps)
 2nd Brigade 35th Infantry Division (XVII. Corps)

---

[1] *N.B.*—The 4th Batteries of these divisions, like the 23rd Regiment (6th E. S. R. Division), left Liaoyang for Fenghuangcheng on the 30th April.

[2] Every E. S. rifle regiment provided a detachment 100 strong (called also a Commando) of Okhotnoki or mounted scouts. They were generally employed with the regiment.

Rennenkampf's trans-Baikal Cossack Division, posted near Liaoyang:
- 4 regiments of Cossacks
- 2 horse artillery batteries
- Amur Cavalry Regiment
- Verchnewdinski Cossack Regiment

Total in and South of Liaoyang:
- 44 squadrons
- 52 battalions
- 162 guns

Lines of Communication:
- Railway troops
- Frontier (or railway) guards, 55 companies
- 55 squadrons and 16 2-gun (pack) batteries.[1]
- 1st Siberian Infantry Division
- Cossack infantry, etc.

The force on the Yalu was distributed as follows:

Russian Eastern Force

1. At Antung under Kashtalinski:
   - 10th Regiment (less 2 companies)
   - 2 Companies 24th Regiment
   - 1 battery
   - 1 machine gun company
   - 400 mounted scouts

2. At Chiuliencheng, Trusoff:
   - 12th and 22nd Regiments
   - 2 batteries
   - 240 mounted scouts

3. At Tientzu:
   - 9th and 11th Regiments
   - 2 batteries

[1] *Cf.* K. E., 39, 40; Anlage, 7, and Conferences, p. 53.

4. From Anpingho to Hsiaopuhsiho, under Colonel Tronkhine:

    11 squadrons Cossacks
    1 battalion 24th Regiment
    1 company 10th Regiment
    1 mountain battery

5. From the Kouwangkou river to Takushan, with patrols along the coast as far as Pitzuvo, General Mischenko's Cossack Brigade:

    11 squadrons Cossacks
    1 horse artillery battery
    21st Regiment

6. Lines of Communication:

    6 companies (24th Regiment)

The extreme front watched by this force was 172 miles. The line of retreat was to be on Fenghuangcheng, except for the right detachment, which was to retire on Haicheng.

The force was commanded by General Zassulich, who seems to have received contradictory instructions, Kuropatkin directing him to merely observe and delay the enemy,[1] Alexieff desiring him to fight. It seems that Alexieff regarded the general situation as satisfactory at this time.[2]

The Position The position selected by Zassulich to oppose the advance of the Japanese 1st Army, had its centre about Chiuliencheng, where he had caused entrenchments to be constructed.

---

[1] G. S., p. 56.   [2] F. v. T., i. 44.

At this point the valley of the Yalu is some three to four miles wide, and consists of a sandy plain broken up into many islands by the branches of the Yalu and Ai rivers. The ground is open, and except for a few trees on the islands and under the banks is destitute of cover. At the confluence of the rivers is a rocky height known as Tiger Hill. From the high ground in rear spurs run down to the river, ending for the most part in knolls 100 to 300 feet in height sloping steeply to the river bank.[1]

Colonel Madritoff's detachment of about 500 men had left Mukden at the end of March, and marched **Madritoff's** via Penhsihu and Saimachi to Kuantien-**Detachment** cheng, and thence into Korea about Chosan. This force was somewhere to the eastward during the battle of the Yalu.[2]

The Japanese, having concentrated at Wiju, set to work to reconnoitre the ground, and most ela-**Preliminary** borate precautions were taken to conceal **Movements** their own strength. The Russians, on the other hand, made no attempt at concealment. By the 25th bridging material was ready. To assist in the reconnaissance of the main stream, Kyuri Island was occupied by a battalion of the guards, and Kintei Island by a battalion of the 2nd Division, on the night of the 25th-26th. The Russians

[1] I. H., i. 89.   [2] J. de S. M., series 10, vol xxvi. 321.

now withdrew from Tiger Hill, but held on to Chukodai.

The reconnaissance of the river was now undertaken; on the 26th and 27th a bridge was built from Wiju to Kintei; this bridge was built only as a blind.[1] On the night of 27th-28th another bridge was built below it, and bridges near Genkado were completed. All the bridges were fired on by the Russians, but not damaged.

Reconnaissances were pushed into the country between the Aiho and the Yalu, and the country found to be passable. The actual point of passage was now fixed at Suikuchin, where an island existed. It was then decided that the 12th Division should cross at Suikuchin, and the attack be delivered by the whole army on the front Chukodai-Salankou. To obtain simultaneity in the attack the 12th Division was to cross on the night of the 29th, and the attack was fixed for the 1st May.

A feint was made on the 25th and 26th by a naval detachment in the direction of Antung.

The Russian detachments opposite Suikuchin had not failed to observe the Japanese movements, and reports were made to General Zassulich, who ordered a reinforcement of the troops in that direction; but the order was countermanded on the 30th.

During the 29th the 12th Division successfully

[1] G. S., p. 58.

passed the river and commenced the bridges; on the same day Tiger Hill was reoccupied by the Russians. During the night of 29th-30th, the artillery of the 2nd Division and a regiment of 4.72 Howitzers, which had landed at Quiempo, crossed to Kintei, and entrenched. The utmost care was taken to conceal the guns. The same night the 12th Division passed the river and commenced its movement westwards in three columns, the left column along the right bank of the river, the centre column on point 955, and the right column, one squadron, one battalion, making a wide turning movement against Chiaochiakou. Kashtalinski opposed the movement with a rearguard of one battalion and one section of artillery, and reported to Zassulich, who ordered him to hold his ground. Meanwhile the guard artillery from Kyuri had driven the Russians from Tiger Hill, and a Russian battery having opened fire from the high ground north-east of Chiuliencheng, on some boats in the river, the mass of guns in Kintei opened fire on, and silenced it.

Russian Disposition On the 30th Zassulich's force was distributed as follows:—

Under General Kashtalinski, holding a position from Chiuliencheng to Yaokou:
    12th Regiment
    1 battalion, 11th Regiment
    1 battery
    8 machine guns.

Left section or left flank guard (Colonel Gromoff) in a position from Makou to Potetientzu:
    2 battalions, 22nd Regiment
    1 battery (less 1 section)

At Chingkou:
    1 battalion, 22nd Regiment
    2 guns

At Antung:
    9th Regiment
    2 battalions, 11th Regiment
    1 battery

General Reserve at Tientzu:
    10th Regiment
    24th Regiment
    1 battery

General Mischenko's eleven squadrons were away to the west, Colonel Tronkhine's eleven squadrons and the mountain battery had retired north from Anpingho, thus the infantry were left to rely on themselves, with some 450 mounted scouts belonging to the various regiments, most of whom were at Antung and Tientzu.

During the bombardment of the 30th the infantry did not occupy the trenches,[1] but the batteries had suffered, one gun being put out of action.

The particular duty of the left section was to cover the left flank of the position at Chiuliencheng.[2]

The general aspect of the position has already

[1] F. v. T., i. 89.   [2] F. v. T., i. 88.

been described, and it is sufficient to add that infantry trenches were placed along the base of the spurs running down to the river, and were badly concealed. Nevertheless the field of fire was magnificent and the position naturally very strong. Lateral communications did not exist, and the tracks to be followed in retreat were bad; the troops from the Chiuliencheng position had orders to utilise that by Liuchiakou, and the reserve the main road to Fenghuangcheng from Antung.

At 8 P.M. on the 30th the 2nd Division commenced to cross, and moving by Oseki and Tiger Hill to Chukodai Island, by daybreak on the 1st were there entrenched, within 2000 yards of the Russian trenches.

The guards reached their ground between the 12th and 2nd Divisions by 5 A.M., the 12th Division being on the line Salankou to a hill west of Litzuyuan. The division had been rejoined by the troops from Siojo.

The reserve (five squadrons, four battalions) was assembled at Kyuri; one battalion escorted the Howitzers on Kintei.

The base at Rikaho was closed, and transports were ordered to await the result of the fight off Antung.

General Kashtalinski, who commanded at Chiuliencheng, received positive orders from Zassulich to hold his ground. All night long the Russians heard the movements of the Japanese.

At 6 A.M. on the 1st the Japanese batteries opened fire, and about seven the order for the simultaneous advance of the three divisions was given. The advance was at once carried out, and on reaching the Aiho the troops came under a hot fire. For a moment they wavered, but rallied and pressed on, though the left flank of the 2nd Division was checked for a space. The inner flanks of the guard and 2nd Division penetrated the Russian front between Yaokou and Makou, and about 8.30 A.M. occupied the Russian trenches, from which the defenders had already withdrawn.

Action commenced

Front penetrated

The accounts of the Russian proceedings are somewhat confused.

Retreat of 22nd Regiment The troops composing the Russian left section, under Colonel Gromoff, found themselves attacked in front by the guard and on the left by the 12th Division.

The extreme left beyond Potetientzu was held by the 5th Company, 22nd Regiment, and between it and Potetientzu the right of the guard division penetrated.

Gromoff thereupon withdrew the isolated company, and about 8.30 A.M. decided to throw back his left, and take up a position on the ridge parallel to the Chingkou road, from which latter place he hoped to be reinforced by the other battalion of his regiment (the 22nd) and a section of artillery. While the section reserve was moving to the position selected on the ridge, the above-mentioned irruption of the Japanese troops between Makou and Yaokou was reported. Gromoff now decided to retire on Chingkou. The battery, turning first one way and then another, was captured by the Japanese Guard.

The Chingkou detachment also found its line of retreat imperilled, and retired about 10.30 A.M., after a sharp action.

Russian Situation at 9.30 a.m. Thus about 9.30 A.M. the Russians' right section had retired in good order, as had the Chingkou detachment. The left section under Gromoff had lost some 300 men and six guns, but were out of danger.

Kashtalinski now occupied a position on the right bank of the Huntuhotzu stream, with the four battalions, the battery, and machine gun battery.

The Japanese at this time were: 2nd Division concentrating with the General Reserve near Chiuliencheng; Guards, on the hills between Yaokou and Potetientzu; 12th Division, left on hill north of Potetientzu, right climbing ridge west of Fangtaitungtzu. The artillery of the 2nd Division was in position on

Japanese Situation at 9.30 a.m.

Chukodai, two batteries close to Chiuliencheng; that of the guards in position between Yaokou and Makou; that of the 12th Division on the right bank of the Aiho; the Howitzers on Kintei Island.

It was 9 A.M. when the Japanese occupied the Russian position, but they did not move forward, possibly because the 12th Division was finding its advance so difficult and slow. At 9.30 A.M., Zassulich ordered the troops at Antung to withdraw on Tientzu, which they did about noon, and about 10 A.M. he ordered Kashtalinski also to withdraw, forming the rearguard to the whole force. To reinforce him two battalions (11th Regiment) and a battery were ordered up from Tientzu, whither they had come from Antung.

About 11 A.M. Gromoff, who was on the saddle on the Chingkou road, was joined by the battalion of the 22nd Regiment from Chingkou, and seeing the Japanese pushing round his left he withdrew, arriving safely on the main road.

About 11.30 A.M., Kuroki directed a pursuit by the reserve along the Hamatang-Fenghuangcheng road, the 2nd Division to move on Antung.

The threat of this advance, which, as a matter of fact, Kuroki had decided not to press, caused Kashtalinski to withdraw, and about this time he for the first time realised that Gromoff was beaten.

The road along which the Russians were retreating runs through a valley bounded by steep and rocky hills. South-east of Hamatang the valley narrows to about 1000 yards, and on the south side of the road is a rocky ridge about 150 feet above it, while on the north side the hills slope steeply to the Huntuhotzu stream. The 1st and 3rd Battalions, 11th Regiment, were now ordered to occupy hill 570, and did so. The battery which accompanied these battalions was ordered to return to the main road. At 2 P.M., just as the wagons of the battery reached the northern mouth of the gorge, they were fired on by Japanese troops. It was the 5th Company, 24th Regiment, of the 12th Division. The wagons escaped, but not so the guns, which, finding escape blocked, came into action to assist the two battalions, 11th Regiment. All efforts of the Russians to drive back the obstinate Japanese company failed, and two battalions of the 4th Guards and one of the 30th Regiment now approached the scene.

The Retreat

Kashtalinski's troops, as they fell back, also came under fire. The battery, the machine gun section, and several companies (probably five) went into action, the remainder of these troops continuing their march and breaking through.

As the ring closed round the doomed remnant, various attempts were made to break out, and a

The Charge of the 11th Regiment
strong attack was delivered by the 3rd Battalion of the 11th Regiment. With band playing and colours flying the battalion went forward to the attack with the bayonet, as they had practised so many many times before on their barrack fields. Their invisible foes, for they do not seem to have crossed bayonets with any of the enemy, lay and fired at them. Many escaped, among them sixteen of the thirty-two bandsmen; these men afterwards received the St George's Cross.

Gradually the Russians on the hill were driven down into the valley, and more Japanese troops came up. The gallant 5th Company still held its own.

The remainder of the 11th, portions of the 12th, and a company of the 22nd Regiment[1] apparently, with the two batteries and eight machine guns, still held out; the men digging themselves into the ground during the engagement. At 5.10 P.M., just as General Watanabe had ordered a company of the 4th Guards to attack with the bayonet, the white flag was shown and the Russians sur-

Surrender of the Rearguard
rendered. This obstinate resistance enabled the main body to withdraw in complete safety on Pienmen. Next day the Russians reached Fenghuangcheng.

[1] The escort of the battery captured near Yinkou which had rallied to the 12th Regiment.

The losses on either side were: Japanese, 1021; Russians, between 2400 and 3000 (of whom 600 were prisoners), twenty-one guns, and eight machine guns.

The general strategical situation required that the Japanese advance should be delayed, and it was for this purpose that the detachment on the Yalu was pushed forward. In the words of Kuropatkin, the detachment was posted "not for a decisive action against the enemy in superior numbers." The action required was similar to that of Ziethen on the Sambre in 1815. The two ways to defend a river line are: 1. To defend all the crossings, which necessitates splitting up the force into fractions. 2. To watch and delay the enemy at the crossings with small bodies, holding a reserve in hand to attack the enemy as he debouches on the defender's bank. Typical instances of this latter operation, are the attack by the Archduke Charles on Lannes and Massena at Aspern, and Lees' attack on Hooker at Chancelorsville. Napoleon has stated that it is impossible to prevent an enemy crossing a river, and the successful passage of the Lower Danube by the Russians in 1877 is a proof of the truth of this assertion. It follows that the second method of defence is the stronger. Up to the 30th July however, the Russian dispositions may be described as fairly sound, if it was not intended to seriously dispute the passage of the river. The Japanese control of the sea made the position of the Russian right precarious. When, however, the Japanese had made good the crossing and turned the Russian left, the time had arrived for a withdrawal, or else a bold offensive against the turning force. If, however, Zassulich was determined to fight a rearguard action, then, in view of the time available, which was ample, the following points should have been attended to:—

1. The position for the rearguard should have been strongly entrenched.

2. A position, or positions, in rear should have been prepared.

3. Good roads should have been constructed and intercommunication arranged.

4. The guns should have been carefully defiladed.

5. Every unit should have been instructed exactly what to do when the time came to retreat.

6. The reserve from Tientzu should have been brought up on the 30th within reach, and strengthened by the bulk of the troops from Antung.

Not one of these points were attended to; in particular the intercommunication, a detail which could have been arranged in a few minutes, was not arranged for.[1] Some use could also have been

[1] Conferences, p. 71.

found for Colonel Tronkhine's eleven squadrons. Two other comments on the Russian dispositions appear obvious; the first is that Zassulich did not reconnoitre, or even appear in person, near Chiuliencheng on the 30th; the other that Kuropatkin, from Liaoyang, interfered in the details of the arrangements of the defence.[1]

General Sir Ian Hamilton, who examined the position closely, is of opinion that the Russian **Tactical Remarks** artillery might have done more by holding back until the infantry attack commenced, and then boldly pushing in to take a part in repulsing it; and he offers as an example the conduct of Hunt's guns at Gettysburg, which were so instrumental in beating off Pickett's great charge, and the Confederates' guns at Fredericksburg.

The Russian musketry proved bad, company volleys being solely employed. The Japanese losses were much higher than necessary, owing to the denseness of their formation—a thick chain of skirmishers and closed company columns in rear.

The moral effect of this first encounter must have been almost incalculable, for it was inevitable that **Moral Effect** up to the last there should be a doubt as to whether the yellow man could face and beat the white.

[1] F. v. T., p. 97.

The Action at Hamatang

The charge of the battalion (11th Regiment) during the fight at Hamatang indubitably took place, and it is indeed unfortunate that no war correspondents were present to record the deed in fitting words. What exactly the battalion attacked is not clear. Those who have seen a modern action will know how difficult it is to locate the enemy, and it is permissible to suppose that the battalion charged a space where there was no enemy, that the Japanese merely thought they were running away, and shot as many as they could before they got clear. The German great general staff draws from this story, the moral that determined troops will always find a way out with the bayonet, even against magazine rifles. The truth probably is that this depends on how well the enemy shoots.

CHAPTER III

EVENTS IN MAY 1904

Disembarkation of the 2nd Army—The Railway interrupted—Movement on Chinchou—1st Army—4th Army—2nd Army—Garrison of Port Arthur—The Nanshan Position—The Battle of Nanshan—Losses—Comments—3rd Army undertakes the Siege—4th Army—1st Army—Russian Operations on the East Front—2nd Army moves North—General Situation end of May

ONE hundred and three transports[1] crowded with troops had been lying at Chinampo awaiting the news of the result of the battle of the Yalu. These transports carried the 1st, 3rd, and 4th Divisions, and an artillery brigade, which were destined to land on the south coast of Manchuria, between Takushan and Talienwan, to cut the communication between Port Arthur and the main Russian army, and advance along the railway against Liaoyang. For reasons connected with the suitability of the coast line, the point selected for the disembarkation was Houtushih, near the mouth of the Tasha river.

Disembarkation of 2nd Japanese Army

[1] B. O. R., i. p. 61.

Elaborate precautions were taken by the fleet to block the approach of Russian torpedo boats. The straits between the Eliott Islands and the mainland were mined and patrolled. On 6th May the disembarkation commenced, and was not interfered with by the Russians, who hurriedly fell back northwards after making a reconnaissance; on the 7th and 8th the 3rd and 1st Divisions occupied a line along the Pitzuwo-Chinchou road from the Tasha to the Shouyi rivers. On the 10th the 4th Division began to land and assemble at Machiatun.[1]

On the 6th a force of the divisional cavalry supported by one and a half battalions had moved at once on Pulantien and cut the railway. It appears, however, that the damage was made good, and the communications were only definitely cut about the 13th.

The Railway cut

There was constant skirmishing, and on the 14th the 1st Division, with a brigade of the 4th Division, moved on Chinchou, and on the 16th attacked the Russian advanced force under General Fock, four battalions and a battery, at Shihsanlitai. The Russians abandoned the heights north and east of Chinchou, but held the town. Thus Oku's army stood on the 20th May: 1st Division and one brigade of the 4th near Chinchou, remainder of the 4th at

Movement on Chinchou

See Map 3

[1] O. R., p. 125.

Pulantien, 3rd Division on the line of the Tasha. On the 15th the disembarkation point had been shifted to about fifteen miles south of Pitzuwo. On the 23rd the 5th Division and a cavalry brigade commenced to disembark.

Meanwhile, on the 4th May, Kuroki advanced towards Fenghuangcheng, occupying that town on the 6th.[1] By the 11th his army was concentrated at that place. On this flank the Cossacks were active.[2] On May 10th[3] Colonel Madritoff, whose movements were referred to in Chapter II., attacked Anju (see Map 3), with some 500 men. He was beaten, and his retreat harried by the Koreans.[4]

1st Army

On May 19th General Kawamura arrived off Takushan with the 10th Division, which was to form the nucleus of the 4th Army, and commenced to disembark near that place.

4th Army

All along the front from near Aiyangcheng to near Takushan there was constant skirmishing with the Cossacks. In order to further embarrass the Russians, a demonstration was made by the fleet near Kaiping, as if to select a landing-place.

At 10 A.M. on the 21st[5] General Oku issued

[1] O. R., p. 118. [2] O. R., p. 119.
[3] J. de S. M., series 10, vol. xxvi. p. 321. [4] O. R., p. 127.
[5] B. O. R., i. p. 64.

orders to his army to concentrate on a line Shihsanlitai - Mount Sampson - Saitzuho.

Operations of the 2nd Army

Each division left a detachment of two squadrons and one battalion. At the same time the G.O.C. 5th Division received instructions to occupy a line from Pulantien along the Tasha river with the cavalry brigade, his own division, and the detachments mentioned, and cover the rear of the army.

The Russians had used the period that had elapsed since the commencement of the war to good

Garrison of Port Arthur

purpose, to push on the work on the defences of Port Arthur, to provide and equip the fortress with every necessary, and to place a very strong garrison at the disposal of General Stoessel, the commander. This garrison consisted of:

>   4th and 7th divisions of East Siberian Rifles complete with the guns (56 pieces)
>   5th Regiment of East Siberian Rifles
>   1 battalion of East Siberian Engineers
>   3 battalions of fortress troops
>   1 battery of 5.7 Q. F. guns
>   1 sortie battery
>   1 company of fortress engineers
>   1 company of fortress miners
>   1 telegraph section
>   Some frontier and railway guard troops
>   Total—35,000. (There were also some volunteers.)

To delay the enemy's advance General Stoessel

had pushed forward the 4th East Siberian Rifle Division (General Fock) with the 5th East Siberian Rifle Regiment and five batteries towards Chinchou, and a strong position had been prepared on the Nanshan Hill south of Chinchou.

Russian Troops at Nanshan

"This position is well illustrated by laying the left hand on the table with the fingers slightly bent and a little apart. On the spurs represented by the thumb and fingers were redoubts with trenches along their front and sides protecting the valleys, while the highest point of the hill is like the knuckle of the middle finger."[1]

The Position

The hill had a command of about 250 to 350 feet over the plain in front. The extent of the position is 3300 yards, and the flank rests on the sea. The field of fire is good, but within 600 yards, particularly on the west side, where the command is greatest, the ground is broken and deep twisting ravines lead in places directly into the position. The road communications are good; two (unmetalled) roads and the railway afford lines of retreat. The hill of Nankuanling affords a good *position de repli*. This position, naturally strong, was most formidably entrenched. Thirty heavy

[1] R. A. I. P., vol. xxxiv. p. 94. Article by Captain Archdale, D.S.O., R.H.A.

guns, of old pattern it is true, but powerful, were mounted in closed works of a semi-permanent character. Lines of fire trenches with zigzag communications were placed in tiers, and all the works, even the advanced works, were closed by shelter trenches. The front and flanks were covered by a network of wire entanglements and a number of naval mines. There were two searchlights. It seems, however, that the trenches and traverses were often badly sited.[1]

To occupy these formidable lines General Fock had available some 13,000 men and eighty guns,[2] and in addition the works near Talienwan, also mounting some heavy guns, could take part in the defence. On the position of Nankuanling only works for the field guns were constructed.

No arrangements were made for a counter-attack. The lines were at present held by the 5th E. S. R. Regiment, a detachment of frontier guards being in Chinchou.

The attack was intended to take place on the 25th, and at 5.50 A.M. the artillery opened fire at Chinchou and silenced the four frontier guards' guns there. The infantry then attacked, but were repulsed.

[1] B. O. R., i. p. 78.
[2] This figure is doubtful. G. S., ii., seems to show sixty-eight guns exclusive of six batteries of Q. F. guns with the 4th E. S. R. Division. Further there were four frontier guard guns and some heavy Howitzers.

The Attack   The co-operation of four gunboats in Chinchou Bay was expected; the weather, however, prevented their arrival. General Oku therefore decided to postpone the attack [1] till next day.

On the evening of the 25th orders for the attack were issued as follows:—[2]

4th Division to move on Chinchou, attack it at midnight, and occupy the south face of the town down to the sea at Chinchou Bay.

1st Division to occupy a line from the southeast corner of Chinchou to Chilichuang, with guns on the right flank and reserve at Tangwangtun.

3rd Division to be by daylight on the line Chilichuang-Hsinchiatun; guns in rear of the left flank.

Russian Distribution   General Fock had distributed his troops on the position as follows:—

On the hill of Nanshan, with a company in Chinchou:

>   5th E. S. R. Regiment
>   Two mounted scout detachments
>   Two companies 9th E. S. R. Regiment
>   Approximately 2700 bayonets

of whom only three and a half companies could form local and general reserves.

On the hill of Nankuanling, the 4th East Siberian Rifle Division.

[1] O. R., p. 133.   [2] B. O. R., i. p. 78.

On the right:
>1 regiment
>1 battery

In the centre:
>1 regiment
>1 battery

On the left:
>1 regiment
>3 batteries (two of the 7th E. S. R. Division attached)

At the junction of the Dalny and Port Arthur railway lines:
>1 regiment
>1 battery

Comment

Such a distribution showed a determination to utilise the strongly-defended position of Nanshan merely as a false front to the position of Nankuanling. Had General Fock had any intention of assuming the offensive at any time, he would have held more than one regiment in his own hand.

Japanese Attack

A furious storm prevented the 4th Division from occupying Chinchou, and therefore the guns of the 1st Division could not get into action. Towards dawn the 1st Division occupied, itself, the town.[1] By 5 A.M. the divisions were in their allotted stations. About 5.30 A.M., when the fog lifted, the guns all along the Japanese line came into action, and by

[1] B. O. R., p. 78.

8.30 A.M. most of the Russian guns had ceased firing. At 9 A.M.[1] the infantry of the 4th Division had gained some ground, and a simultaneous attack was made, without firing until 600 yards from the position,[2] and by 10.30 A.M. the troops had pushed close up to the foot of the slopes of the hill. The guns now advanced to closer range. About 6 A.M. the Japanese gunboats from Chinchou Bay were able to assist the attack; a Russian gunboat and the Talienwan forts taking part in the defence.

Half a battery from Nanshan retired to the hill south of Ssuchiatun, whence they could fire on the right of the 4th Division; two more batteries shortly withdrew to the Nankuanling Hill. The 1st Division, which had advanced up close to the obstacles, found itself hard pressed, and was reinforced from the general reserve at 10.30 A.M.[3] The 3rd Division, enfiladed by the Russian gunboat and a battery of field guns near Talienwan, was very severely handled. About this time the Japanese gunboats, which the ebbing tide had forced to retire out of range, were able to again take part in the attack.

Nevertheless bodies of gallant men dashed forward to the obstacles again and again, only to leave

[1] B. O. R., i. p. 79.   [2] B. O. R., i. p. 80.
[3] B. O. R., i. p. 71.

two-thirds of their numbers lying on the bullet-swept ground. All day forward and backward swept the lines of battle, charge after charge was met and repulsed. As the day wore to evening, and every man had been set in the firing line, report after report reached the general that no more could be done, and that ammunition was running short, but still he refused to call off his men, and right well did they justify his confidence. As the sun was setting, the 4th Division in a last effort succeeded in working round the enemy's left, wading through the sea; a trench was enfiladed, men were able to swarm into some of the ravines on this flank, and at about 6.30 P.M. the Russians were forced to retreat.

As the fire of the machine guns ceased and the rifle fire slackened, the 1st and 3rd Divisions dashed forward over the obstacles, and by 7.30 P.M. the Japanese flag was floating from the summit of the hill, while a long line of artillery of the 4th Division, pushing forward in pursuit, was firing on the crowds of men retreating on Nankuanling Hill.

Advance to Nankuanling At 8 P.M. Oku issued orders to bivouac on the captured position. On the 27th a brigade occupied the abandoned Russian position on Nankuanling Hill.

On the 29th the army again advanced, and on the 30th entrenched a position west of Dalny.

Operations to clear the harbour of Dalny of mines were at once begun.

After the battle Fock had retired his troops to the fortress, leaving a weak observation line about **Russian Action** five miles west of Dalny. The Russians occupied this line in some strength on the 30th.[1]

The losses in the battle of Nanshan were: Russians, 850; Japanese, 4324. The Japanese captured some guns, variously estimated **Losses** from eighty-two[2] to thirty.[3] The Japanese official report says sixty-eight.

The battle does not prove that a frontal attack against a fortified position is impossible, yet it was **Comments** to the menace on the flank that the Russians actually yielded. The only reinforcements sent up by Fock to Nanshan were the bulk of the 12th East Siberian Rifle Regiment to reinforce the right—this was done about 9 A.M.[4] —and two and a half companies 14th East Siberian Rifle Regiment, sent up too late to the left.[5] Thus at the end of the day Fock still had under his hand three regiments, and at least sixty-eight field guns, of which forty-eight at least were quick-firers. This disposes at once of the usual criticism, which appears in many continental authors' works, that a reserve should have been held in hand.[6]

[1] K. E., 37, 38, p. 43.
[2] B. O. R., i. p. 76.
[3] Immanuel, p. 115.
[4] G. S., ii. 23.
[5] G. S., ii. 25.
[6] Meunier, p. 113, etc.

The statements that Stoessel himself conducted the battle seem quite wrong,[1] and even Fock only arrived during the morning.[2] The picture of the confusion, the orders and counter-orders, the marching and counter-marching, of the Russian troops previous to the battle, as drawn by Nojine, is most remarkable. For example, the 15th East Siberian Rifle Regiment was sent back to Port Arthur on the 20th and back again to Nanshan on the 24th. Seeing that the Russians had had more than three months to elaborate their arrangements, this seems peculiar. The quarrelling and jealousy among the senior officers of the troops under Stoessel, coupled with their incompetency in many cases, were no doubt largely responsible for the Russian failure. Little more than 3000 men, with eighty or ninety[3] guns, held the Japanese 35,000 and 198 guns fast all day. There is little doubt that General Fock lost such a chance as seldom can occur. No doubt his orders were explicit that he was not to expose more men than necessary, but one can well imagine how one of the great subordinates of former wars would have acted—a Lannes, a Davout, a Manteuffel, a Von Werder, a Hill or a Crawford, a Jackson or a Sheridan.

[1] Löffler, i. p. 50.   [2] Nojine, p. 70.
[3] Perhaps more.

Three battalions sent forward on the left to repulse the attack of the 4th Division, while on the right the remaining six battalions, advancing in a strong line of battle against the 3rd and 1st Divisions, already exhausted and short of ammunition, would surely have carried all before them, and the whole Russian force of 12,000 to 15,000 bayonets, supported by the fire of eighty guns, would have reached the batteries, would have captured the pieces, and, if urged forward as Stonewall Jackson would have urged his men, would have so dealt with Oku's troops that the victory of Nanshan would have revenged the rearguard defeat at Hamatang, and have altered the whole aspect of the war. But "It was the characteristic of the Russian leadership that throughout the war it never found the right way of escape from the defensive attitude which it adopted almost of its own free will."[1]

With regard to the tactics of the battle, the great value of machine guns in the defensive is **Tactical Comments** to be remarked, and also the fact that the Japanese artillery, although they specially sought to do so, did not locate and silence them.

The 198 guns of the 3rd Army were controlled by the commanding artillery officer stationed on

[1] K. E., 39, 40, p. 144.

a small but commanding hill (near H.Q.).[1] The enemy's position had been carefully reconnoitred, and sketches made of it and of the positions to be occupied by the guns. These sketches were distributed to the batteries.[2] It is understood that this system of command did not have the desired effect.[3] However that may be, the concentration of the Japanese fire on battery after battery in turn seems to have been the means by which the Russian pieces were silenced.[4]

The position of the Russian Howitzers on the top of the hill seems curious.[5] The air lines of the telephones in the Russian position which connected the batteries were destroyed early in the battle;[6] thus intercommunication was impossible.

Landing of the 3rd Army

While the action at Nanshan was taking place the 11th Division had begun landing at Yentai Bay. Their transport was not landed till 3rd June; but as the cavalry brigade to the north, near Wafangtien, was in touch with Russian cavalry in some strength, Oku decided to call the 11th Division up to him at once.

The 1st Division was left with the 11th in the

[1] See Map.   [2] Geddes, p. 34.   [3] *Ibid.* p. 45.
[4] Nojine, p. 68.   [5] I. H., ii. p. 325.   [6] Nojine p. 69.

lines in front of Dalny, and formed the nucleus of the 3rd Army, under command of General Nogi. To him was entrusted the siege of Port Arthur, with the following troops:—

>1st, 11th, and 9th Divisions
>1st and 4th Reserve Brigades
>1 field artillery brigade
>1 heavy artillery regiment
>A siege train
>Fortress engineers, etc.

Talienwan Bay was cleared of mines, Dalny used as a base.[1]

It is now necessary to return to the eastern side of the theatre of war. The 10th Division, which formed the nucleus of the 4th Army, was ordered to mobilise on the 16th April, and on the 19th May commenced to disembark at Kuchiatun, a place some twenty miles south-west of Takushan. The beach was an open one, and the foreshore, as is the case all along the Manchurian coast, is at low tide a large expanse of mud flats. A party of blue-jackets 500 strong landed first, and under cover of them the troops began to disembark. By the evening of the 19th the whole 20th brigade was ashore, and the transport, cavalry, and guns were landing at a pier

The Disembarkation of the 10th Division

[1] O. R., p. 140.

constructed in two hours by the harbour master and his staff.[1] It was not till the 10th June, however, that the division complete was ashore.

The troops opposing the Japanese at this point consisted of a brigade of Cossacks supported by a regiment of infantry, under Mischenko, with headquarters at Hsiuyen.

No attempt was made to disturb the landing, but on the 20th a force pushing forward from Kuchiatun to occupy Takushan came in contact with some Cossacks, surprising a squadron and inflicting heavy loss on them near Wankiatun. A screen was formed round Takushan, and the disembarkation proceeded with. Constant skirmishing took place, and on 25th May the advanced troops of the 10th Division moved up to Koulienho. Takushan was utilised as a base.

To assist the 10th Division Kuroki stretched out to right and left; a mixed brigade of the 12th **Movements** Division occupied Aiyangcheng on the **of 1st Army** 28th of May, after a sharp engagement.

After the battle of the Yalu, Rennenkampf was despatched with instructions to watch the extreme **Russian** eastern flank of the army, to guard **Operations** against a march of the Japanese 1st Army direct on Mukden. Marching via Langtzushan, he reached the neighbourhood of Saimachi

[1] B. O. R., i. p. 108

on the 7th May[1] with Ljubavin's Cossack Brigade. Here he was joined by the 23rd E. S. R. Regiment and a field battery, and also by eight squadrons and two mountain guns. His force then amounted to twenty squadrons, three battalions, eight field, six horse, and two mountain guns.

Between Rennenkampf's troops and the Japanese there was constant skirmishing, but the Cossacks were unable to pierce the screen of the Japanese lines, for Japanese infantry occupied all the passes and the Cossacks could make no headway. Small parties on foot, larger parties mounted, were equally unsuccessful, and when Rennenkampf wanted information he was obliged to obtain it at the head of a strong force.[2] The first serious engagement took place with the mixed brigade of the 12th Division, already referred to, near Aiyangcheng. It was the result of a reconnaissance from which "little was gained except that Kuantiencheng was held by the Japanese, and it is worthy of note as illustrating Russian methods at this stage of the war, that, though Aiyangcheng was still held, no troops were left there to watch the movements of the Japanese."[3]

Dismounted Cossacks obliged the Japanese advanced guard to deploy, but were soon themselves forced by the mountain artillery of the 12th Divi-

[1] K. E., 41, 42, p. 54. [2] K. E., 41, 42, p. 55. [3] G. S., ii. 95.

sion to retire. On the 29th Rennenkampf withdrew from Saimachi, leaving a regiment of Cossacks on the Paliling Pass. His infantry had already gone back to Chiaotou, and he reported to Count Keller, the commander of the East Detachment, that strong Japanese forces were in occupation of Saimachi.

On the 16th May General Count Keller arrived in Langtzushan to take command of the East Detachment. He found work on "positions" covering the passes already in progress, and formidable works were being constructed to cover the approach to Langtzushan. As Freiherr von Tettau points out, the position itself was strong, but there was room enough in the mountains for the Japanese to go round it.[1] Keller found his troops distributed over an immense length of road:

3rd. E. S. R. Division	8 battalions 20 guns in Langtzushan
	2 battalions 12 guns on the Motienling Pass and in Tawan
	1 battalion on the Fenshuiling Pass (1)
	1 battalion near Erhtaotangshan
6th E. S. R. Division	3 battalions and a battery supporting Rennenkampf at Chiaotou
	3 battalions in Tawan
	3 battalions and a section on the Modulin Pass
	3 battalions (21st E. S. R.) and a battery on the Fenshuiling Pass (2) supporting Mischenko

[2] F. v. T., pp. 125, 126.

Mischenko, at Hsiuyen, was further supported by a regiment (18th E. S. R.) on the Fenshuiling Pass (2) sent from Haicheng by the II. Corps. Ten squadrons of Cossacks available, besides Rennenkampf's troops, were distributed on the various roads leading from the south and south-east to Langtzushan and Tawan; the remaining squadrons of these regiments being employed as orderlies, guards, etc.

Comment The troops of the East Detachment were therefore on all the southern roads, covering a front of fifty-five miles and distributed in a depth of three days' march.[1]

Towards the end of May, Keller decided to clear up the situation in the direction of Fenghuangcheng, and on the 29th May made his reserve at Langtzushan close up to the front to Lienshankwan. The 2nd Brigade 2nd Siberian Infantry Division, IV. Corps, was ordered by Kuropatkin to Langtzushan in support of the movement.

Keller decides to advance

On receiving Rennenkampf's report of the 29th, and further one from the regiment left near Saimachi, on the 31st Keller decided to march on Saimachi instead of Fenghuangcheng.

It is noticeable that the Russians were constantly worried about the road to Mukden via Saimachi.

---

[1] K. E., 41, 42, p. 56.

This reconnaissance will be described in the next chapter.

Movements of 2nd Army On 31st May Oku's troops turned northwards, and on the 3rd June the cavalry, now near Telissu, reported strong bodies of Russian infantry at that place.

At this point it is necessary to examine the general situation. The Japanese forces were placed at the end of May:—

General Situation

On the right, 1st Army about Fenghuangcheng, with detachments at Aiyangcheng. Three divisions and probably a reserve brigade.

In the centre, 4th Army somewhat advanced from Takushan. At present only one division, which was completing its disembarkation of transport stores, etc.

On the left, 2nd Army about Pulantien. Three divisions, a cavalry brigade, and a field artillery brigade.

3rd Army, 1st and 11th Divisions holding a position in front of Dalny, covering the concentration of the army at that port.

Russians East Detachment: Count Keller as outlined above. Twenty-three squadrons, thirty battalions, seventy guns.

I. Siberian Corps: Yinkou, Kaiping, and Tashichiao. Thirty-two battalions, seventy-two guns.

H.Q. with II. Siberian Corps and part IV. Siberian Corps: Liaoyang to Haicheng. Eighteen squadrons, forty-four battalions, 118 guns.

Mischenko's Cavalry Brigade: Hsiuyen; with two regiments and a battery on the Fenshuiling Pass (2) in support, sixteen squadrons, six battalions, fourteen guns.

In front of the I. Siberian Corps a brigade of cavalry, twenty-two squadrons, and six guns, under Samssonoff, was at Telissu already in touch with the Japanese cavalry.

There were small detachments in North-East Korea, at Hsinmintun, and in the valley of the Liao river, amounting to some twenty squadrons and a few companies.

The remainder of the IV. Siberian Corps was in transport on the railway. Exclusive of troops for lines of communication and fortresses, this gives an available strength of some 7000 sabres, 142,000 bayonets, 290 guns.

Liaoyang was being rapidly turned into a fortified camp of the strongest nature. Works were being constructed at Kaiping, Tashichiao, Hsimucheng, Shoushanpu, Anshanchan, Anping, etc., and in fact on all the roads leading to Liaoyang.

The Russian love of "positions" was given free play.

CHAPTER IV

EVENTS IN JUNE

Intentions of Russians—Cavalry Actions on South Front—Orders to I. Siberian Corps—Comments—Russian Movements — Japanese Movements — Telissu — Advanced Guard Action—Battle of Telissu—Comments—4th Army advances—Movements on East Front—General Japanese Advance—Rennenkampf attacks Aiyangcheng—Count Keller's Reconnaissance—1st Army advances—4th Army advances—Occupation of the Passes—Comments—General Situation at end of June—Port Arthur

WHEN Alexieff returned from Port Arthur early in May, he proceeded to urge on Kuropatkin the advisability of a forward move against the Japanese. It would seem that Alexieff favoured an attack on Kuroki,[1] but that this was rejected by Kuropatkin on account of the lack of transport. Kuropatkin apparently did have some idea of moving south against Oku in full strength, but the reports from the east front caused him to change his mind, and as we have seen he despatched a brigade to the support of Count Keller. Still, pressure from Alexieff and

Intentions of the Russian Commander

[1] Conferences, p. 121, and G. S., ii. 30.

St Petersburg made it imperative to do something, and so towards the end of May, General Baron Stakelberg was ordered to concentrate the I. Siberian Corps towards Telissu.

On the 30th[1] Samssonoff's cavalry, reconnoitring in the direction of Telissu, was in touch, and **Cavalry Engagements** a sharp engagement took place, during which occurred practically the only cavalry charge of the war. Two sotnias of Cossacks surprised, charged, and drove back a squadron of Japanese cavalry. The supports and machine guns placed in a village stopped the pursuit; two more Japanese squadrons then attempted to attack the Cossacks in flank, but were themselves driven back by the fire action of the supporting sotnias. Finally the advance of the Japanese infantry supports forced the Cossacks to fall back.

On the 1st June the 1st East Siberian Rifle Division arrived at Telissu. On the 3rd there was another indecisive cavalry engagement, but the Japanese discovered the presence of Russian infantry[2] in force. The Japanese cavalry retired to Wafangtien after the engagement of the 3rd, and was followed on the 7th by the Russian cavalry, now commanded by Simonoff.

Stakelberg's troops were advancing steadily by road and rail, and on the 7th he received the fol-

[1] O. R., 144.   [2] K. E., 41, 42, p. 5.

Orders to General Stakelberg lowing direction: "To you and your detachment is assigned the duty of moving towards Port Arthur and drawing on itself the greatest possible number of the enemy, thus weakening the attack on the Kwantung peninsula. For this purpose your movement against the Japanese forces sent northwards must be swift and energetic, in order to keep in view the surprise of the advanced detachments. A battle, however, is not to be delivered against superior strength, and the reserve is only to be used when the situation is entirely cleared up. Your final aim will be the capture of the Chinchou position and the relief of Port Arthur."[1]

The meaning of this order cannot be described as clear. It is quite impossible to say whether or no Kuropatkin really meant to attempt the relief of Port Arthur. On 4th May Kuropatkin had learnt the Japanese dispositions,[2] and thus knew that Oku had a strong force at Pulantien, probably the 5th and 11th Divisions; he could not therefore really have expected Stakelberg to find only weak forces in front of him. It seems very much as if Kuropatkin was trying to make the best of a bad job which had been forced on him, and the clause in his instructions that Stakelberg was not to fight against superior strength

Comments

[1] K. E., 41, 42, p. 6.   [2] K. E., 41, 42, p. 6.

would, it might be hoped, bring him safely back to Kaiping very shortly.

Distribution of the Russian Troops — On the 7th June the troops of the I. Siberian Corps, or South Detachment, as it was now called, were distributed as follows: —

Wafangtien: Simonoff with 14 squadrons and a battery

Telissu:
2 squadrons
4 frontier guard guns
1st E. S. Rifle Division
36th E. S. Rifle Regiment (9th E. S. R. Division)
2 companies, 1st E. S. Sapper Battalion

Kaiping:
2 battalions, 33rd E. S. R. Regiment (9th E. S. R. Division)
3 batteries (9th E. S. R. Division)

Tashichiao:
1 battalion, 33rd E. S. R. Regiment (9th E. S. R. Division)

Yinkou:
34th E. S. R. Regiment (9th E. S. R. Division)
1 battery (9th E. S. R. Division)

Haicheng:
35th E. S. R. Regiment (9th E. S. R. Division)
2nd Brigade, 35th Infantry Division
1 horse artillery battery
3 field batteries (35th Infantry Division)

The troops at Yinkou and Tashichiao were to be relieved by the 3rd East Siberian Rifle Division, and then join Stakelberg; but a Japanese naval demonstration at Kaiping on the 7th June caused a temporary suspension of their movement south.[1]

It appears that the orders of the 7th were repeated and enlarged in orders of the 8th and 11th, but their exact purport is not known.[2]

On the 10th June one brigade of the 1st East Siberian Rifle Division at Telissu was pushed on to Wafangtien in support of the cavalry.

On the 12th the advanced posts of both sides were in close touch on a line south of this place.

On 12th June Oku's army, concentrated at Pulantien for some days, had at last been completed with transport, and the casualties of Nanshan had been made good by fresh drafts.[3] The divisions, therefore, broke camp, and moved northwards: 3rd Division up the valley of the Tasha river, 1st Division and 1st Field Artillery Brigade (less one regiment) along the railway, 4th Division and one regiment field artillery along the Mandarin Road to Fuchou.

Japanese Movements

The 6th Division commenced disembarking at Kerr's Bay on the 13th June, and received orders to push up troops as available in support of the movement northwards. On the 13th the Russian advanced troops slowly gave way.

Stakelberg had spent some days[4] in examining

[1] K. E., 41, 42, p. 5.
[2] K. E., 41, 42, p. 6.
[3] B. O. R., i. p. 93.
[4] K. E., 41, 42, p. 7.

the ground near Telissu (the point he had been directed to concentrate on), with a view to selecting and defending a "position." Work on the position had begun on the 9th.[1]

The Position at Telissu

The position selected was some three miles south of the village of Telissu, and was about three and a half miles in extent.[2] The right flank rested on some low hills, with a narrow valley in front; the centre was across the valley of the Fuchou stream and the railway, the left was on some low but steep hills, on a spur of which called Lungwangmiao was the main Russian gun position. The field of fire was poor, particularly on the left, and here some redoubts had been constructed. On the right the infantry entrenchments were shallow pits nine inches deep with low parapets some fifteen inches high.

South of the position and about 2000 yards from it is a ridge about 600 to 1000 feet in height which completely shuts in the view to the south. Through a gap in this ridge runs the river and the railway. From Lungwangmiao to this gap the range is about 1500 yards.[3]

It is to be noticed that if the Japanese could

---

[1] K. E., 41, 42, p. 7.   [2] B. O. R., iii. p. 85.
[3] R. A. I. Proceedings, vol. xxxiv. p. 93. Article by Captain Archdale, D.S.O., R.H.A.

occupy the hills on the right near the village of Tafangshen, the gun position at Lungwangmiao could be enfiladed. North of the position the valley gradually narrows as far as the village of Telissu.

A portion of the 9th East Siberian Rifle Division only arrived during the night of the 14th-15th.

Respective Forces For the battle of the 15th Stakelberg was able to concentrate some thirty-two battalions, nineteen squadrons—that is, a total of 27,000 bayonets and 2500 sabres and ninety-eight guns. Further reinforcements arriving during the battle of the 15th brought the total up to about 30,000 bayonets and 100 guns. The Japanese force of one cavalry brigade, three divisions, one artillery brigade, amounted to some 2000 sabres, 36,000 bayonets, 216 guns.

Distribution of Russians For the defence of the selected position Stakelberg distributed his troops as follows:—

Right Section—36th E. S. R. Regiment, one and a quarter battalions 33rd E. S. R. Regiment, one and a half companies engineers, one battery, on the heights north and east of Tafangshen.

Centre Section—Three-quarter battalion 33rd E. S. R. Regiment, four batteries, thence to the railway.

Left Section—Four squadrons, 1st East Siberian

Rifle Division, five batteries, half company engineers, from the railway eastwards.

Reserve—At Telissu station, 2nd Brigade, 35th Infantry Division, two batteries.

The cavalry was to cover the right flank, and keep communication with the detachment in Fuchou, and send three squadrons to the left flank on the 14th June.

During the early morning of the 14th June Simonoff received orders which apparently gave him to understand that resistance south of Telissu was not intended.[1] When, therefore, the Japanese advanced on the 14th, he gave way before them, and in the afternoon was north of Hsialungkou. The cavalry appears to have lost touch with the enemy, but nevertheless it made certain of the fact that Japanese troops were in the Fuchou valley south-east of Ssuchiatun. The orders to keep touch with the detachment in Fuchou and send three squadrons to the left of the position were certainly not carried out.[2] The eastern (left) section was occupied as follows:—On the right 4th East Siberian Rifle Regiment and three batteries; next to them 3rd East Siberian Rifle Regiment on a ridge, with four guns on the left flank. 1st East Siberian Rifle Regiment as reserve on the slope north of Wafangwopu on the road to Tsuichiatun. The 2nd

14th June Advanced Guard Action

[1] K. E., 41, 42, p. 16.   [2] K. E., 41, 42, p. 17.

East Siberian Regiment and the 4th Battery of the division were behind the 3rd Regiment; one squadron and a scout detachment watched the outer (left) flank.

Japanese Advance

The advanced guard of the 3rd Division (one regiment and four batteries), meeting no opposition in the morning, in the afternoon occupied the heights north of Ssuchiatun, and the batteries went into action north-west of the village against the conspicuous Russian guns on the Lungwangmiao spur. This led to a severe cannonade, which reached its height about 3 P.M. Two more batteries reinforced the advanced guard batteries of the 3rd Division, and during the cannonade the whole of the Russian batteries disclosed their positions. A most careful reconnaissance was made, particularly by the 5th Division.[1] This latter did not bring any guns into action, except one battery east of Pachangchientzu in support of the 3rd Division.

About 4 P.M.[2] two regiments of field artillery (seventy-two guns) also came into action, but about 7 P.M. the firing died away, and the troops bivouacked on the ground as follows:—4th Division about Hsiaossuchiatun, 5th and 3rd Divisions on a line Sungchiatun-Wangchiatun-Wuchiatun, cavalry at Shabaotzu.

[1] K. E., 41, 42, p. 19.   [2] B. O. R., i. p. 84.

During the engagement the 2nd Brigade 35th Infantry Division from Telissu station was moved up behind the Russian left and reached Tsuichiatun (east), placing one battalion and four guns at Feichiatun and two battalions and four guns in the Wafangwopu valley.[1]

General Oku came to the conclusion, as a result of the reconnaissance made during the advance guard action of the 14th, that the Russian force was something less than three divisions, and that troops were constantly arriving by train.[2]

The following orders for the attack next day were therefore issued at 11 P.M. from the Japanese headquarters:—

Orders for the Attack
1. The 5th Division will advance before dawn from the neighbourhood of Wuchiatun and attack the enemy at Tafangshen, but will delay its further movement up the Fuchou valley.

2. The 3rd Division, keeping touch with the 5th Division, will advance as soon as the latter has begun its attack.[3]

The G.O.C. 4th Division received instructions as follows:—" As no danger is to be anticipated from the direction of the valley of the Fuchou river, you will detach a force of at least one brigade of infantry to-morrow, which will attack

[1] Conferences, p. 140. [2] G. S., ii. 40. [3] B. O. R., i. p. 38.

the enemy's right flank and help the advance of the other divisions."

The cavalry was instructed to cover the right flank, and was reinforced by one battalion and one battery from the 3rd Division.

Thus the Japanese commander had decided to hold the Russian in front, outflank him on both wings, and crush his right.

General Stakelberg, although he is stated to have been an advocate of the Russian system of "position" actions,[1] had no intention of retiring without a fight. On the 12th he had had an interview with Kuropatkin, but the orders issued then are not known, except that Stakelberg received permission to concentrate his whole force, part of which was still at Kaiping. It seems certain that the general was ignorant of the fact that a whole Japanese division was on his right,[2] and therefore considered the situation to be cleared up. The orders for the next day were therefore based on a serious misapprehension of the situation. In two "directions" to General Gerngros, commanding the 1st East Siberian Rifle Division, Stakelberg directed that an attack should be delivered against the Japanese right. For this purpose the centre section, where the artillery of the 9th East Siberian

Russian Dispositions

[1] B. O. R., iii. p. 85.   [2] K. E., 41, 42, §p. 21.

Rifle Division, under General Mrosovski stood, was strengthened by a regiment and two batteries of the 1st East Siberian Rifle Division. To support the attack the 2nd Brigade 35th Infantry Division, commanded by General Glasko, was ordered to report to Gerngros; it was reinforced by one battalion 34th East Siberian Rifle Regiment. Thus a force of eighteen battalions and thirty-two guns out of a total of only thirty-two battalions and ninety-eight guns was to deliver the counter-attack.

During the night the rest of the 9th East Siberian Rifle Division arrived, and also four squadrons and a horse artillery battery. The four squadrons were sent to General Glasko. At daybreak on the 25th the centre section, astride the railway, was occupied by thirty-six guns—twenty east and sixteen west of the railway—with the 4th East Siberian Rifle Regiment and three companies 33rd East Siberian Rifle Regiment.

The right section was held by two regiments 9th East Siberian Rifle Division (less five companies), who had two and a quarter battalions in front line and one and a half battalions 36th East Siberian Rifle Regiment as local reserve.

On the left the three regiments of the 1st East Siberian Rifle Division were formed for attack; 2nd and 3rd Regiments in first line, 1st in reserve in a small wood. Glasko with the 35th Infantry

Brigade, complete, one battalion 34th East Siberian Rifle Regiment, and four batteries, stood behind the left. As general reserve were 35th and 34th (less one battalion) East Siberian Rifle Regiments and one horse artillery battery near Telissu, stationed in a small wood.

The Japanese had moved off between four and five o'clock,[1] but there was a thick fog shrouding the field of battle in the early hours of the 15th. About 5.30 A.M. the weather cleared and the Japanese artillery at Wangchiatun (a) opened fire. More guns came into action on their left and left rear. The troops of the 3rd Division, awaiting in their shelter trenches the result of the bombardment, saw the Russians in front of them increasing in numbers, for the counter-attack was impending.

The Battle

The 2nd Brigade 35th Infantry Division had not come up, but General Gerngros decided, nevertheless, to attack, awaiting their support. The overpowering weight of metal had already enabled the Japanese to nearly silence the Russian batteries on Lungwangmiao, and they were free to turn their attention to the attacking infantry. Nevertheless the attack was strong, and well pushed home, in spite of the fire, the steepness of the slopes, and the heat, and by about ten o'clock the firing line

[1] K. E., 41, 42, p. 21.

was within 600 yards of the Japanese shelter trenches.

About 7 A.M. the artillery of the 5th Division was in action on the north bank of the Fuchou river, and the infantry had reached a line Yangchiatun-Wangchiatun (b). As the firing on the right was very heavy, the division prolonged its line to the left By 10 A.M. the Russians had been forced to abandon the height east of Tafangshen and the Japanese were firmly established there.

5th Division

The guns of the division (mountain artillery) now advanced to the height just captured, while two regiments of the Field Artillery Brigade came into action near Wangchiatun (b) against the Russian artillery at Lungwangmiao.

The Japanese 19th Brigade, a squadron, and a battalion of artillery of the 4th Division, arrived at Yangchiatun at 9 A.M., and at 9.30 A.M. reached the heights south-west of Machiafanghsin. Seeing that the Russian right was in the air, the main body of the 4th Division detached a party to intercept the Russian retreat.[1]

4th Division

On the Russian left the attacks on the heights south of the village of Ssuchiachou were still being most gallantly pressed. Charge after charge was attempted, and one or two

[1] O. R., p. 154.

men succeeded in reaching the trenches. On account of the ground on this flank the Japanese divisional artillery could be of little service at first, but about 10 A.M. the advance of the 5th Division had enabled some guns to get forward. At noon Oku was able to send forward one of his two reserve battalions (one of the 6th Division having arrived [1]), and the cavalry brigade, dismounting, proceeded to strike in to the attack in the direction of Feichiatun, though under severe artillery fire. Meanwhile on the Russian right the steady advance of the Japanese was carrying all before it. The local reserve had formed front to the west to meet the attack of the Japanese 19th Brigade (4th Division), and General Stakelberg sent the 34th and 35th East Siberian Rifle Regiments and a battery of the 35th Infantry Division, and also the horse artillery battery, to the right wing. The reserve was replaced by four battalions 9th Siberian Infantry Regiment which had opportunely arrived by train. The 19th Japanese Brigade occupied the heights southeast of Tunglungkou between 11 A.M. and noon, but could not advance further rapidly. Stakelberg in person proceeded to the right with two battalions 35th East Siberian Rifle Regiment and the horse artillery battery, to try and check the Japanese. Gradually the Rus-

[1] K. E., 41, 42, p. 22.

sians were again outflanked. One battalion of the 9th Infantry Regiment had been sent to Samssonoff, but the other three were sent up about noon. The horse artillery battery succeeded in enfilading the left of the Japanese 19th Brigade, but could not stop the advance. By 12.45 p.m.[1] the battle was obviously lost, and orders for the retreat were issued.

The retreat of the right was skilfully and successfully accomplished, the last troops being clear about 2 p.m. The brigade of the 35th Division was ordered to form a rearguard and cover the retreat of the 1st East Siberian Rifle Division. It received these orders about 2 p.m.[2] The orders to Gerngros, however, had to be taken by an orderly over four miles of bad ground.[3] About 1 p.m. the 4th East Siberian Rifle Regiment, which had been with the guns near Lungwangmiao, had retreated, whether with or without orders is not certain.[4] About 1.30 p.m. Gerngros had given orders to the rest of the division to withdraw, but it was a difficult and slow operation. The 3rd Division was now advancing, about 3 p.m. the cavalry reached Feichiatun, and a line of guns took position on Lungwangmiao. In their retreat Gerngros' troops lost heavily from shell fire, as they retired down the valley.

[1] B. O. R., iii. p. 86.　　　[2] K. E., 41, 42, p. 25.
[3] B. O. R., iii. p. 87.　　　[4] K. E., 41, 42, p. 23.

Shortly after 3 P.M. a tremendous thunderstorm broke, which completely covered the Russian retreat and prevented a pursuit.

The action of the 2nd Brigade, 35th Division, has been purposely left to the end. General Glasko did not consider his orders of the night of 14th-15th clear, and sent orderlies to headquarters, and also to General Gerngros, to ask for explanations. Gerngros replied that an attack was hopeful, and at 6.40 P.M. General Glasko, the commander of the brigade, gave orders to advance. He had detachments on the pass south of Feichiatun and south of Tsuichiatun (East); he reinforced each of these by a battalion and ordered them to advance, the former on Chiochiatun and the latter on Wafangwopu. The reserve three battalions and two batteries followed the advance on Wafangwopu. At this time Gerngros again sent a message, "Strike in, we will support you from the heights."[1] About an hour later a direction from headquarters to Glasko arrived worded as follows: "In the case of an attack in superior force against our centre or in any other direction, the I. Siberian Army Corps will slowly retire on Wantselin. The detachment Glasko will in this case hold as long as possible the line East Tsuichiatun-Kousiatun,[2] in order to cover the retirement of the

Marginal note: Proceedings of the Brigade, 35th Division

[1] K. E., 41, 42, p. 24.   [2] Not on Map. Not identified.

column which passes by Telissu through the defile at West Tsuichiatun." Then follow directions about the retreat.

At 7 p.m.[1] the advance on Wafangwopu was brought to a standstill, and the enemy's cavalry was reported active on the left. The sound of the battle on the right grew momentarily more severe. Glasko supposed that Stakelberg's expected case of "an attack in superior force" had arrived, and ordering his advanced troops to hold their ground, he proceeded to take up a position with his reserve on the line East Tsuichiatun-Kousiatun.[2] After a time he came to the conclusion that his movement was over-early.

At 10 a.m. a general staff officer from headquarters arrived and ordered Glasko to attack at once. He reinforced his advanced troops—two battalions and two batteries on the right, one battalion and one battery on the left. The right advance was soon again brought to a stop, and the guns could not advance because of the ground, while the left column was assailed by the dismounted cavalry, under cover of fire from machine guns and the battery attached to the cavalry brigade, and was brought to a standstill.

At 2 p.m. Glasko received orders to form the

[1] K. E., 41, 42, p. 25.
[2] Not on map. Not identified.

rearguard. Retiring steadily, the brigade reached East Tsuichiatun about 5 p.m.[1]

A Cossack Regiment ambushed

The small detachment, from the main body of the 4th Japanese Division referred to above, ambushed a body of six squadrons near Chiaochiatun.

The Russians retreated in three columns, and marched all night, reaching Wantselin station on the morning of the 16th. The cavalry, under Samssonoff (vice Simonoff invalided), had followed the rearguard and took up feeling with the enemy again next morning.

Russian Retreat

Losses

The Japanese lost 1163; the Russians 3481[2] and sixteen[3] guns.

The original instructions given to General Baron Stakelberg have already been quoted, but without knowing the further orders given by Kuropatkin, and in particular the result of the conference on the 12th, it is impossible to be sure what General Stakelberg's final orders were. It would seem, however, that it had been decided to offer battle. For the first time we find a Russian general standing in a defensive position and yet determined to deliver a counter-attack. In this connection it is interesting to compare "Combined Training," p. 122. "A commander who intends

Comments

---

[1] K. E., 41, 42, p. 25.   [2] U. S. Official Reports.
[3] B. O. R., i. p. 90.

to fight a decisive action on a defensive position should particularly keep in view the defence of his line of retreat and the preparation of the counter-attack." Although "Combined Training" lays down this principle, it is very far from suggesting that the "defensive-offensive" attitude is one to be adopted from choice; and it is historically true, that with the possible exception of Austerlitz, no modern battlefield has shown an example of a successful battle fought under such a general idea. The successful counter-strokes of history have been unpremeditated, and their success has as a rule been due to the tactical insight of the general, or the arrival on the field of another body of troops. It has been suggested that Stakelberg should have acted offensively on the 14th.[1] In view of his orders this suggestion, however, appears untenable. It seems quite clear that after the engagement of the 14th Stakelberg had no idea of the presence of the 4th Japanese Division on his right flank. Either he was not informed by his cavalry, or if news was sent in it was not believed, or was not reported to the general.[2]

However that may be, Stakelberg held that the position was cleared up by the action of the 14th. His reserve was ordered up in the rear of the

[1] Conferences, p. 144. [2] See B. O. R., iii. p. 86.

left, and a new reserve built up out of the fresh troops arriving. It can hardly be doubted that if Glasko had struck in boldly on the 15th the right of the 3rd Japanese Division would have been forced back. The situation would then have been somewhat similar to that of Bragg and Rosecrans at Murfreesboro on 31st December 1862.

The Japanese operations were of a singularly simple and direct nature. The front and flanks were to be assailed and the right flank of the Russians enveloped. It has been said that the employment of only a fraction of the 4th Division was not a masterpiece of determined leading on the part of General Oku. It should be remembered, however, that Kuropatkin had about Haicheng a very large force, and that this force might be coming up. It was to guard against such a move that the remainder of the 4th Division was employed. The advanced-guard action of the 14th was a typical action, as described in "Combined Training," section 110 (1).

The movement of the main body 4th Division was slow; had its advance been more energetic it might have intercepted the line of retreat of the Russians. It would seem that on this occasion the action of the Cossacks was successful in at any rate delaying the Japanese movements.

An instance of bad staff work on the Russian

side is mentioned by the British attaché. About 3 p.m. a train of transport wagons arrived, and caused some confusion before they were turned about and withdrawn.

The position selected by General Stakelberg was weak in several important features. Lateral communication was difficult, and the screen of hills southward enabled the Japanese to concentrate unseen; it was, however, probably as good as could be found.[1] Should, however, the high ground by Tafangshen be lost, the Japanese would be able to enfilade the main gun position on Lungwangmiao.[2]

Comments

The field works were, it seems, in some cases very conspicuous,[3] but in other cases care was taken to conceal them.[4]

All accounts of the action unite in attributing the result very largely to the Japanese artillery. The engagement of the 14th enabled the Japanese to locate the Russian batteries very accurately; they were also assisted no doubt by secret service agents.[5] They then carefully selected their own positions. The skilful use of ground by the Japanese infantry has also been commented on, for instance their employment of the woods on the right bank of the Fuchou river.

[1] B. O. R., iii. p. 84.
[2] B. O. R., i. p. 91.
[3] B. O. R., i. p. 91.
[4] B. O. R., iii. p. 84.
[5] B. O. R., i. p. 84. Meunier and others,

When news of Stakelberg's projected movement south had been received at headquarters in Tokio, and it had been decided to send the 2nd Army to meet it, the following direction was sent to Kawamura: "Your division will hold itself in readiness to advance on Kaiping at any moment. With this object it will collect as much transport and supplies as possible, at points as far north as is practicable in the district which it now occupies." The first step, then, for the 10th Division was to occupy Hsiuyen.[1]

Two roads lead from Takushan to Hsiuyen; one along the valley of the Tayang river, the other direct. This latter was the one selected for an advance.[2] On 3rd June Mischenko took the offensive and attacked the Japanese advanced troops near Koulienho, but without success. On the 6th June a mixed brigade of the guard division from Fenghuangcheng occupied Shalisai, under cover of the 10th Divisional Cavalry, which had moved into the valley of the Tayang river. Mischenko had already withdrawn to Hsiuyen, and occupied a position south-east of that place.

4th Army

Support by 1st Army

On the 8th June an attack on Mischenko's position was delivered from the south and east. The south attack did not make much headway, but the eastern attack jeopardised

Occupation of Hsiuyen

[1] G. S., ii. 68. [2] O. R., 128.

the Russian line of retreat, and they fell back in some haste, covered by a rearguard. There was no pursuit. It will be observed that this success was due to the careful preparation of a simultaneous converging attack by superior numbers.

As previously mentioned in Chapter III., on the 30th May Count Keller received permission from headquarters to lead a reconnaissance towards Saimachi. The road from Lienshankwan to Saimachi runs along narrow stony valleys, and is really only a seldom-used track.[1] The force actually taking part in the movement was only six battalions and two batteries; two other battalions reconnoitred towards Fenghuangcheng. On the 1st June[2] the force moved, and on the same day the advanced guard reached Saimachi after a twenty-seven mile march in appalling weather; the main body was some miles in rear. Keller had intended to proceed towards Aiyangcheng next day, but at Saimachi he received a telegram from Kuropatkin recalling him to watch the passes.[3]

Eastern Detachment offensive Reconnaissance

The only result of this expedition was said by

[1] F. v. T., i. p. 143. [2] F. v. T., i. p. 145.
[3] F. v. T., i. p. 148.

General Kashtalinski to be 8000 pairs of boots ruined.[1] The reconnaissance towards Fenghuangcheng was also fruitless.

Comments

On the 5th June Rennenkampf, who had moved to Saimachi, had a sharp engagement with the Japanese on the Aiyangcheng road. He then retired, leaving a detachment at Saimachi, which was attacked on the 7th by a Japanese force of one squadron, one regiment, one section artillery. The Russian detachment consisted apparently of two squadrons, one battalion 22nd East Siberian Rifles, and a battery. Colonel Grekoff, commanding the Russians, had occupied a position on a ridge a quarter of a mile north of the town. The fire trenches were sited about twenty-five yards down from the crest of the ridge but had no communication trenches. About 10 P.M. the Japanese guns opened the action, and about 1 P.M., when the Japanese infantry were within about 1000 yards, Grekoff retired, pursued for some distance by the Japanese.[2]

Japanese forward Movement

This movement of the Japanese was part of a general advance towards the passes of all the advanced troops in front of Kuroki's army. Its strategical effect has been already remarked. Count Keller ordered Gre-

General forward Move

---

[1] F. v. T., i. p. 150.   [2] B. O. R., i. p. 136.

koff, with the whole 22nd Regiment, to retake Saimachi; but this movement, begun on the 11th, was given up, as the Japanese evacuated that place.[1]

Forward Movement stops
The general forward movement of the Japanese stopped, and it seemed clear that a general advance was not yet to take place. On 17th Rennenkampf reoccupied Saimachi, and on the 21st moved from there with six squadrons, one infantry regiment, a horse artillery battery, and four mountain guns[2] against Aiyangcheng.

Engagement at Aiyangcheng
The Japanese position at this place was naturally strong, was entrenched with great skill,[3] and had a good field of fire. About 10 A.M. on the 22nd Rennenkampf drove in the outposts, but was unable to deliver an attack against the very superior force of Japanese in the main position till about 2 P.M. His attack was frontal, and foredoomed to failure. About 5 P.M. the Russians withdrew in some confusion to Saimachi. The Japanese did not pursue.

There is no doubt that Rennenkampf's information was faulty, but the action served as a reconnaissance in force, and cleared up the situation.

Comment

After the battle of Telissu, and the movement

[1] K. E., 41, 42, p. 58. [2] K. E., 41, 42, 59.
[3] B. O. R., i. 139.

of the 10th Division and a brigade of Guards to Hsiuyen, Kuropatkin expected a rapid movement of the Japanese towards Liaoyang. On 14th June Keller was therefore ordered to send six battalions and a battery to Haicheng, and on the 15th yet another six battalions followed. The 5th East Siberian Rifle Division from Liaoyang was called up to Haicheng, and the detachment on the Fenshuiling Pass (2) was increased to four regiments; a regiment was sent to the Chipanling Pass to support Mischenko. The available troops of the IV. Siberian Corps were already at Haicheng. However, the Japanese did not advance, on account of supply difficulties. Kuropatkin then seems to have thought of moving south against Oku, and the troops at Haicheng actually moved towards Kaiping on the 26th June, but were brought back again to near Tashichiao.

General Situation of Russians

On the 17th June Keller made another offensive reconnaissance towards Fenghuangcheng, this time with a force of three squadrons and some mounted scouts, one battery, eight battalions, and a half company of engineers. The Japanese advanced posts were driven back on their supports, but nothing was found out; the weather was terrible, and every track a swamp. On the 19th the troops were in their old positions on the passes.

Second offensive Reconnaissance by Count Keller

Comment

The complete failure of the Russians on this flank to obtain any information of the Japanese movements is most interesting. The Japanese mixed detachments of infantry and troopers were able to keep all efforts at bay. Yet the Russian mounted troops on the east front were strong, amounting to at least twenty-three squadrons, not counting mounted scouts or men employed as orderlies, etc. The Japanese cavalry were only eight squadrons. It would appear that here was a chance for a bold and enterprising leader of light horsemen, even in the mountainous country of Southern Manchuria.

1st Army Advances

On the 25th June Kuroki had at last got his transport in working order and supplies accumulated for an advance. The main body broke camp and marched that day from Fenghuangcheng in three columns. On the right—remainder of 12th Division, via Taitzushan and Erhtaohotzu; centre column—2nd Division and Headquarters, via Erhtaofangshan; left column — remainder of Guards division, via Tahuangkou and Erchchiaputzu.

On the 31st the 2nd Division occupied the Motienling Pass without much resistance, for the advance of the Guards had outflanked the Russian line of positions. Keller's troops withdrew, detachments occasionally fighting rearguard actions.[1]

Count Keller's action had been crippled by Kuropatkin's indecision. Regiment after regiment had been taken away and then sent back. Just as the Japanese advanced the 9th East Siberian Rifle Regiment was withdrawn from the East Detachment. As an instance of indecision, the 12th East Siberian Rifle Regiment was ordered to Anshanchan on 15th June and at once sent back to Count Keller. On the 26th it was sent to Tawan, and while on the march ordered to return to its old camp, which it reached at 1 A.M.

On the 31st the army stood: 12th Division part Aiyangcheng, part a little west of the Paliling Pass, which was held by the Russians; 2nd Division occupying the passes near the Motienling, with a reserve at Lienshankwan; Guards (less Asada's Mixed Brigade) near Erchiaputzu, with advanced troops on the Modulin Pass, connecting with the left of the 2nd Division; Army Headquarters at Lienshankwan. The great success and perfect timing of this march is to be noted. The cavalry was employed to keep open the communication between the columns.[2]

Apparently part if not all the Guard Reserve Brigade was on the road from Shuitien through Kuantiencheng to Aiyangcheng.

[1] K. E., 41, 42, p. 60.   [2] G. S., ii. 100.

The 10th Division also advanced on the 24th June. Its advanced detachments had already been active, and had threatened the Chipanling Pass on the 18th. On the same date Mischenko had withdrawn to the Fenshuiling Pass and the Japanese occupied his positions. To cross the formidable main range in front of them the Japanese had a choice of several roads; of these the chief is that by Fenshuiling, and this the Russians had defended in a most formidable manner. It was decided by General Kawamura to manœuvre the Russians out of this position, and for this purpose he divided his troops into four columns and a reserve as follows:—

Advance of the 4th Army

Right Column—Asada:
  Guard Mixed Brigade 2 batteries and 1 company engineers in addition.

Total
  2 squadrons
  6 battalions
  4 batteries
  2 companies engineers

No. 2. Column—Kamada:
  1 squadron
  1 battery
  2 battalions
  1 section of engineers

No. 3. Column—Marui:
  2 squadrons
  1 battery
  4 battalions
  1 section engineers

No. 4 Column—Tojo:
    1 squadron
    2 batteries
    4 battalions
    1 company engineers
Reserve:
    1 squadron
    1 battalion

Just as he was starting on the 24th, Kawamura received news from Port Arthur that the attack there was postponed, and from the 2nd Army that their advance was checked for want of supplies; but he held to his purpose, and the movement continued.[1]

Orders for the Advance
The right column was to occupy the high ground north of Wangchiaputzu on the 26th.

No. 2 Column from Lichiaputzu (*a*) was to attack the Russian right from the direction of Tasanpihuo.

No. 3 Column was to occupy the heights west of Chiehkuanchin on the 26th. On the 27th it was to occupy a ridge some two and a half miles north of this point with a detachment, and move the main body against the Russian line of retreat.

No. 4 Column worked still wider on the left, to attack Mischenko.

The reserve was to be at Wangchiaputzu.

The troops on the Fenshuiling (or Dalin) Pass

[1] K. E., 41, 42, p. 34.

were commanded by General Levetsam, and now **Russian Disposition** consisted of three[1] infantry regiments, three batteries, and a regiment of Cossacks. General Mischenko with his brigade of Cossacks and one infantry regiment was to the westward, in the direction of Hsienchiachokou. Levetsam distributed his troops as follows:—on the right of the road five companies and a battery; on the left three companies and a battery; in reserve, seven companies. In advance of the position were three and a half squadrons and a battalion, towards Siandiasan on the extreme right were two companies and a squadron, and on the extreme left one company and a half squadron. Care was taken to connect all the parts of the position by telephones, heliographs, orderlies, etc.[2] As a second line a battalion and a squadron were placed at Hsiaoukshan, two battalions and four guns at Yanglahuo, one battalion and four guns on the Panling Pass.[3] Two companies apparently remained with the baggage.

On the 26th No. 4 Column, advancing in two columns, met the bulk of Mischenko's force west **Japanese Advance** of Hsienchiachokon, but was unable to advance; on the 27th the attack was

---

[1] The 18th E. S. R. Regiment which had been with Levetsam had returned to its division.
[2] K. E., 41, 42, p. 36.   [3] Not on map.

resumed, but was unsuccessful, though a large force of Russians was thus held fast.

No. 3 Column had much difficulty in opening communication with No. 4, but on doing so discovered its predicament, and then rendered it some assistance by attacking the enemy on the hills near Chouchiachang. The attack was successful.

On the 27th Marui resumed his forward movement, and though bad roads and the weather prevented his action being decisive, the pressure of his column against the Russian line of retreat near Lamufang undoubtedly greatly helped the main action.

The right column, after sharp fighting, reached its position on the 26th, and sent a regiment on a wide flanking movement to the north.

During the night of 26th-27th two battalions 8th Regiment and a battery arrived at Hsimucheng **Russian Arrangements** and were placed by General Levetsam at Tadoku and Hsimucheng.

On the 27th columns Nos. 1 and 2 resumed the attack; the timely arrival of the **Japanese Attack** regiment sent out on the 26th against the Russian left while No. 2 Column arrived on the Russian right, forced the enemy to withdraw. General Levetsam began this operation about 9.30 A.M., withdrawing by successive sections. No. 2 Column had reached its destination only after sharp fighting, following a trying night march. After assisting in the attack, this column pursued the Russians, and moving with great difficulty by a rough track along the southern slopes of the Tihuangshan[1] mountain, were able to pour a heavy fire into the retreating enemy.[2]

The retreat of the Russians from the Fenshuiling (or Dalin) Pass endangered Mischenko's left, and about 7 P.M.[3] he also withdrew, followed by the Japanese advanced troops.

The losses on either side were slight.

The operations of the 26th and 27th secured for the Japanese the passage of a difficult mountain barrier strongly defended. "It was accomplished by holding the enemy in front and throwing well-timed detachments against his front and rear."[4]

Comments

Thus at the end of July the chief passes from the south and south-east into the plain of Liaoyang were in Japanese hands, and a long pause in the operations took place while the communications were organised. The forces on either side were distributed as follows (Map VIII.):—

General Situation

Japanese:

1st Army:

12th Division—covering the right of the Army
2nd Division—Lienshankwan and Motienling Pass

---

[1] Not on Map.   [2] B. O. R., i. p. 118.
[3] K. E., 41, 42, p. 35.   [4] B. O. R., i. p. 119.

Guards—Modulin Pass

Guard Reserve Brigade—on the Saimachi-Chiaotou road

4th Army:

10th Division—on the Fenshuiling Pass

Guard "Mixed" Brigade—at Hsiuyen

2nd Army:

3rd, 4th, 5th Divisions—Hsiungyaocheng

6th Division—in rear

3rd Army:

outside Port Arthur

Russians :

South Front:

Kaiping.—I. Siberian Corps

    Samsonoff's Cavalry Brigade

    28 squadrons, 24 battalions, 62 guns

Haicheng, Tashichiao, and Yinkou.—IV. Siberian Corps

    6 squadrons, 33 battalions, 160 guns

Tangchih.—Mischenko's Cossack Division

    1 division infantry
    1 brigade infantry
    28 squadrons, 22 battalions, 72 guns

Hsimucheng.—II. Siberian Corps

    12 squadrons, 15 battalions, 46 guns

East Front:

Chiaotou—Rennenkampf's detachment—

    19 squadrons, 5 battalions, 26 guns

Tawan, Chiaotou and Langtzushan.—Detachments in the passes with supports in rear

> About 2 divisions
> 5 squadrons, 18 battalions, 48 guns [1]

Liaoyang.—Headquarters

> 15 squadrons, 5 battalions, 12 guns

In movement on railway:

> Part X. Army Corps
> Part XVII. Army Corps

At Mukden, Kirin, Harbin, and L. of C. in Manchuria:

> dêpot and railway troops
> 20 squadrons
> 13 batteries

Vladivostok.—under Linevitch:

> 27 squadrons, 22 battalions, 64 guns

Port Arthur

Outside Port Arthur the Russians and Japanese remained for some time in the positions taken up at the end of May, the Japanese covering Dalny and the Russians working on their lines and the fortress. The Russian right centre rested on a mountain known as the Houyanshan, and the whole position lay from shore to shore across the peninsula.

Nogi considered this position dangerous to Dalny, for the Russians were superior to him in numbers. He therefore ordered the 11th Division, covered on

---

[1] *N.B.*—The 21st E. S. R. Regiment, which had been detached to the Fenshuiling Pass, had returned to Keller.

the right by the 1st Division, to capture the Houyanshan mountain.

On the night of 25th-26th the 11th Division moved forward in three columns. It seems that the Russian lines were very weakly held. The right column was entirely successful; the left column had no success, and its flank was attacked by Russian gunboats. To the centre column fell the task of taking the Houyanshan mountain itself.

It seems to have been defended by seven companies and a battery, who succeeded in holding the Japanese back all day and inflicting serious losses on them. At last, however, the guns, having pushed in to 2000 yards,[1] silenced the Russian battery, and when two batteries of the right column were able to enfilade the Russian infantry trenches, the Japanese attack succeeded; about 5.30 P.M. the Russians withdrew. No attempt whatever at counter-attack was made by the Russians; the left section of their line was never attacked. The section attacked seems to have only been held by one regiment.

This little action must have shown the Japanese what a resistance they would meet with in attacking the main works of the fortress. A bold offensive by Stoessel in the afternoon with a whole division would probably have thrown back the 11th Division, and temporarily endangered Dalny.

Comments

[1] K. E., 37, 38, p. 45.

CHAPTER V

Events in July

Port Arthur—Distribution of Russian Forces on East Front—Night Attack on Motienling—Attack on Motienling, 17th July—Japanese occupy Chiaotou—Kawamura advances—Oku advances—Battle of Tashichiao—Comments—4th Army advances—Russian Position at Hsimucheng—Battle of Hsimucheng—Comments—Advance of X. Corps—Battle on East Front, 31st July—Comments—Situation after Engagements of 31st July—Port Arthur

Stoessel had at first accepted the position created by the Japanese advance of the 26th June. How-
Port Arthur ever, having given his enemy plenty of time to entrench himself, he decided to retake the Houyanshan mountain.

About 1 p.m. on the 3rd July a Russian battery came into action against the troops holding the mountain, and about 5 p.m. a second battery opened fire, and several attacks by infantry, probably three or four battalions, were attempted, some of which were made in close order with bands playing and all the accompaniments of an old-time battle.[1]

[1] K. E., 37, 38, p. 46.

During the night 3rd-4th several attacks were attempted by small parties. On 4th July the attack was resumed, and this time a whole division at least was employed. The Russian rifle fire forced the Japanese artillery to withdraw farther back, and about 6 P.M. the last Japanese reserve was put into the firing line. Still the Russian attack was pressed, and but for a terrible thunderstorm might have been successful.

In the evening the 1st Reserve Brigade from Dalny reinforced the Japanese, and the Russians had to discontinue the attack. On the 5th they withdrew to their original position.

Comments

The fight of the 3rd seems to have been a reconnaissance preceding the desperate and well-conducted battle of the 4th. The Russian infantry seem to have fought remarkably well, in spite of their close formations.

Events in the main Theatre

Kuropatkin had hurried to Hsimucheng on hearing of the loss of the Fenshuiling Pass; but on the 30th June he returned to Haicheng. He brought up to that point part of the X. Corps, which had begun to arrive; but, with the exception of the 2nd Brigade 31st Division and three batteries, he sent these troops back to Liaoyang on the 7th July. The 2nd

Brigade 35th Infantry Division, the 2nd Brigade 31st Infantry Division, and the 5th East Siberian Rifle Division were placed at Hsimucheng and Haicheng. The IV. Siberian Corps remained at Tashichiao, the I. at Kaiping.

Distribution of Russian East Detachment Count Keller had evacuated the passes in front of the line of the Lan river, and gone back to the ridge behind that stream with troops on the passes and reserves at Tawan and Langtzushan. A detachment occupied Chiaotou. The cavalry (Rennenkampf's Division) was north of the Taitse river.

On the night of 3rd-4th July the Russians attempted to recapture the Motienling Pass. Two battalions attacked the outposts about **Night Attack on Motienling** 4 A.M. on the 4th; one battalion attacked the New Temple, some 800 yards north of the Old Temple, overran the piquet, and nearly reached the support, when it was checked by a reconnoitring party of twenty men sent from the New Temple. At the same time a company from the Old Temple, skilfully moving under cover of a ridge just northward of the line of the Russian attack, took the battalion in the left flank. The Russians formed to the left to meet this attack, and were then taken in flank by the reconnoitring party, who had fallen back to the edge of the wood.[1]

[1] I. H., i. 237.

The Russians now retreated, followed by the Japanese, who had been reinforced. The other Russian battalion, which had been directed on the Old Temple, fell back on seeing the failure of the attack on the New Temple. Had the attacks been simultaneous, they would almost certainly have succeeded.[1]

As the Japanese on the south front appeared to be inactive, Kuropatkin decided to utilise his available troops to support Count Keller, and therefore despatched to his support the 9th Division (X. Corps) directly it detrained at Liaoyang. It was disposed: one brigade and three batteries at Tawan, one brigade and three batteries at Chiaotou. Rennenkampf's Cossacks were in the direction of Penhsihu.

Count Keller reinforced

In the middle of July Keller requested leave to attack the Motienling, and received permission to make a reconnaissance, but not with the view of recapturing the passes.[2] For the attack, which he ordered for the 17th July, he detailed three columns:—

Main Column—Fourteen and a half battalions, one battery, four mountain guns.

[1] I. H., p. 240. [2] K. E., 41, 42, p. 62.

Right Flank Guard, to move against the Hsinkailing Pass—One battalion.

Left Flank Guard, to move against the Japanese near Hsiamatang—Three battalions, half a squadron.

Reserve at Tawan—Apparently twelve to fourteen battalions, nine batteries.

The roads which debouch into the valley of the Lan river were held by the Japanese 2nd Division, distributed as follows:—

Japanese Disposition
At Hsiamatang: 16th Regiment (less one battalion)
On the Motienling Pass: 30th Regiment
On the Hsinkailing Pass: 4th Regiment
At Lienshankwan Headquarters: 29th Regiment and the divisional troops

Telephone communication was established.

Southward, with advanced troops on the Lanholin Pass, lay the Guards' Division (less a mixed brigade attached to the 4th Army).

Facing Chiaotou was the 12th Division. At this place were now posted a brigade and four batteries of the 9th Division (X. Corps), under General Herschelman, with some Cossacks attached.

On the night of the 16th-17th Count Keller advanced, with the evident intention of surprising the Japanese. About midnight the piquets, one company 4th Regiment,

The Russian Attack

in advance of the Hsinkailing Pass, were attacked by the leading company of the Russian battalion. Both sides reinforced one another, and a desultory skirmish lasted all the 17th. The 4th Regiment was assisted by a battalion of Guards. The Russians fell back on Makoumentzu.

The alarm was sent by telephone to all the outposts of the division.

About 4 A.M. the advanced guard of the Russian centre column occupied the two temples without resistance. The Japanese had occupied the crest of the ridge, placing two battalions and two batteries in action, and holding one battalion as a local reserve. The Russians continued to advance. On the right they succeeded in working up to within 300 yards of the Japanese left.[1] Their left, however, remained in the Old Temple.

The third Japanese battalion was put into action, with the exception of one company, but the Russians kept receiving reinforcements.

About 8 A.M. heavy masses of the Russians were seen coming up, one battalion moving in column to support the Russian left. This battalion was caught by the Japanese artillery, and lost 300 men in a very few minutes.[2] This loss checked the Russian efforts on their left, and about 8.30 A.M.

[1] I. H., i. p. 268.
[2] I. H., 269.

Japanese reinforcements appeared on the Russian left, and enfiladed their line at long range.[1]

At 9 A.M. the Japanese artillery, which had been firing on a ridge north of the Old Temple, turned their fire on to the Temple itself, and at 9.10 A.M. the Russians retreated. All this time their field battery had been in a position of readiness near Lichiaputzu. Some companies of the 22nd East Siberian Rifle Regiment from the reserve occupied a ridge to check the general Japanese advance.

The pursuit was not pressed very far, for the Japanese were in inferior force. It was not till 2.10 P.M. that the Russian artillery came into action and fired against the troops on the Hsinkailing. The fire ceased about 4.30 P.M. The Russians remained in position in front of Lichiaputzu till next morning.

Action on the Japanese Right

On the Japanese right the action took the following course. The 16th Regiment, which occupied the pass, was ordered to send one battalion to assist at the Hsinkailing, three companies were on outpost on the roads to Chiaotou, Anping, and Tiensuitien.

About 3 A.M. the force was warned of the action at Hsinkailing, but it was 11.40 A.M. before it was

[1] G. S., ii. p. 103, says, "By this time (soon after 8 A.M.) the strength of the Japanese holding the pass had been increased to three regiments, and that of the Russians to four regiments." It is not clear where three Japanese regiments came from.

attacked[1] by two battalions and some cavalry approaching from the direction of Chiaotou. The company on this road fell back on to its main line of defence. Here it was reinforced by a company of pioneers from the General Reserve of the division.[2] At 8 A.M. two Russian battalions from the direction of Anping attacked the outpost company on that road, and succeeded in seizing a high wooded height, which dominated the Japanese position. At 9 A.M. this outpost company was reinforced by two more companies. At the same time the company on the southern road was attacked. Just as this company was about to retire, it was reinforced. The Russians now fell back, and occupied a ridge. Meanwhile the Russians continued to attack the companies on the Anping road. About 1.30 P.M. a Japanese battalion from the General Reserve arrived. About 4.30 P.M. the Russians withdrew. There was no pursuit.

The Russians were tired after a long night march, but it is evident that they were very exactly informed as to the position of the Japanese outposts. The non-employment of their artillery is inexplicable.

Comments

The action was no doubt intended as a reconnaissance in force, but even so the distribution is incomprehensible. A frontal attack has but little

[1] I. H., p. 259. [2] I. H., p. 260.

chance of success in mountainous country, but on the other hand a flank attack has much in its favour. To distribute the force, therefore, as Keller did appears quite unsound. It is also impossible to say why he kept so strong a reserve. Possibly he had been told not to employ the two regiments of the 9th Division (X. Corps) unless necessary.

Sir Ian Hamilton, who was an eye-witness of the battle, makes the following comments:—

1. The Russian officers exposed themselves unnecessarily.

2. The Russian method of fire was section volleys.

3. The men were placed at close interval, without reference to cover.

On the other hand his praise of the gallant bearing of the Russians is expressed in glowing terms, and he says: "It is passing strange that soldiers so steady and formidable in retreat should be so slow and sticky in the attack."[1]

Sir Ian seems further of opinion, that with a proper disposition the attack would have been successful in temporarily dislodging the Japanese.[2]

Profiting by the moral effect of the victory at the Motienling on the 17th, Kuroki ordered the 12th Division to occupy Chiaotou.

Advance of Japanese Right

The Russian "position" was a strong one against the east. It consisted of a

[1] I. H., p. 278. [2] I. H., i. p. 277.

low ridge with an abrupt slope overlooking the valley of the Hsi river. On the other hand the dead ground from the artillery position was considerable.

The Russian force consisted of one brigade, 9th Division (X. Corps), commanded by General Herschelman, four batteries of field and one of mountain artillery, and one regiment of Cossacks.

General Inouye, who commanded the 12th Division, moved forward on the 18th, and by evening the outposts on both sides were in touch. Half the 16th Regiment (2nd Division) was to reinforce the 12th Division.

There was a sharp musketry and artillery action on the evening of the 18th. During the night the Japanese artillery occupied their positions, and the morning opened with an artillery duel. The Russians at first suffered heavily, but after a time found the range, and as the Japanese had expended two-thirds of their ammunition and the Russians had suffered heavily, about 9 A.M. the artillery fire died away.

Meanwhile the infantry had been advancing from their position on the Chiaotou ridge. About 7 A.M., seeing that a frontal attack was impossible, Inouye despatched a regiment to turn the Russian right. It had to make a detour of twelve miles or more, and was supported by a battalion and a half of the

16th Regiment. As Inouye had been obliged to detach two companies to the north to guard against an attack from the direction of Penhsihu, practically no reserve remained in hand.

The frontal attack was pressed boldly; three separate advances in thick lines of skirmishers were made.[1]

Herschelman had covered his right with a battalion, but when the Japanese turning movement made itself felt, seeing himself outmatched, about 2 P.M. he withdrew his artillery. Inouye at the same time ordered his artillery to advance. About 4 P.M. the Russian flank guard began the withdrawal, and about 5 P.M. the crest of the ridge was reached by the Japanese, who pursued the Russians with fire.

The commander of the turning column, seeing the Russians assembling about 3000 yards behind their position, was able by an unperceived movement to get on their line of retreat and inflict a heavy loss on them.

There are only two points of much interest in this little action. First, the skilful use of cover by the Japanese artillery, which enabled thirty-six mountain guns to equal forty Russian guns of very superior power. Secondly, the fine marching of the force which turned the Russian right.

Comments

[1] Meunier, 140.

After this engagement Kuroki stood fast for some time, but movements were continued by the 4th and 2nd Armies. The advance of these armies had been brought up against the series of strong Russian entrenched positions from Yinkou through Tashichiao to Hsimucheng. The main position was at Tashichiao, and was occupied by the I. and IV. Siberian Corps (less 1st Brigade, 2nd Siberian Infantry Division) with Mischenko's and Kossakowski's Cavalry Divisions, the whole commanded by Zarubaieff.

Early in July Marshal Oyama arrived from Japan at Kaiping, and took command of the Japanese forces. He was accompanied by General Kodama, a brilliant soldier, whose reputation both as a soldier and an administrator (he had been Governor of Formosa) stood most extremely high. The relations of these two men to one another appear to have been most happy.

Arrival of Marshal Oyama

At the end of June the 2nd Army had occupied the Russian lines at Hsiungyaocheng, but was unable to continue its advance up the railway until sufficient stores had been accumulated, for at present the railway itself was

2nd Army Advances

not usable. At last the army advanced, and on the 7th July the advance guard drove the Russian rearguard from the hills about a mile south of Kaiping, and it was seen that the Russian position was a very strong one, and covered a front of almost seven miles. The ground in front of the position was open, and on the night of 8th-9th Oku moved his army across the open ground, and on the 9th about 7.30 A.M.[1] an enveloping attack was delivered. But the Russians had already vacated the position and retired on Tashichiao. From the 10th to the 22nd the army remained halted, holding a line north of Kaiping while transport arrangements were being perfected. The railway was now employed as a tramway, the wagons being man-handled. Junks also were used to land stores near Kaiping, to which town they were transported by Chinese carts. Constant skirmishes took place along the front.

Russians Retire

To assist the advance of the 2nd Army Kawamura had been ordered to demonstrate in the direction of Kaiping. The demonstration was made by two columns, one of a "mixed" regiment and one of a "mixed" brigade, which moved in the direction of Tangchih. They were easily contained by the Russians, but had the desired effect of keeping Mischenko idle.

4th Army Advances

[1] B. O. R., i. 94.

On the 15th Mischenko made a reconnaissance with eight squadrons, one and a half battalions, and a battery in the direction of Tangchih, and established the fact that the Japanese were not in force in this direction.

On the 20th Oku issued orders for the advance against the Russian position at Tashichiao. On **Battle of Tashichiao** the 22nd heavy rain caused a postponement of the movement till the 23rd.[1]

The position occupied by the Russian force under Zarubaieff was a strong one.

The Russian Position The right, which was close to the railway, rested on a hillock called Niuhsinshan, and a village called Tienchiatun, both of which were strongly entrenched and protected with obstacles. To the left of this village is a slight hill east of the village of Wangmatai, also strongly entrenched, and behind this were placed five of the eight batteries of the I. Corps, one other being on the right and the remaining two with the reserve. East of this there is a considerable hill, rising some 180 feet above the plain. The western portion of this hill and the ground to the westward was held by the I. Siberian Corps. Eastward of this as far as the Tapingling Pass stood the IV. Siberian Corps. East of this again was Mischenko with a brigade

[1] B. O. R., i. 96.

of Cossacks and two and a half battalions. The reserve, consisting of three regiments and two batteries, was in rear of the centre at Huangtassu. The extreme right was watched by Kossakowski's Cavalry Brigade.

A second position had been roughly prepared in rear of the right flank.[1]

On the right the ground is open and dotted with villages. At this season the plain is covered with the *kaoliang*, now about six feet high. In front of the left is a tangled jumble of hills of no great height, but with steep gullies and ravines. The Russian force present was:

I. Siberian Corps:
24 battalions
8 batteries
3 companies engineers

IV. Siberian Corps (less 1 brigade):[2]
24 battalions
3 batteries
3 companies engineers

Kossakowski:
26 squadrons
12 guns

Mischenko:
28 squadrons
12 guns

[1] Journal U. S. I. of India, vol. xxxvi. p. 287. Article by Captain Archdale, D.S.O., R.H.A.

[2] IV. Siberian Corps consisted of 2nd and 3rd Siberian Infantry Division with regiments of four battalions each.

In round numbers:
  5000 sabres
  30,000 bayonets
  112 guns

To oppose this Oku's army consisted of:

  4 divisions
  1 cavalry brigade
  1 artillery brigade
Probably about:
  2400 sabres
  45,000 bayonets
  252 guns

On the morning of the 23rd the Japanese advanced. On the right the 5th Division, next to them the 3rd Division, then the 6th on the main Kaiping-Tashichiao road, and on the left of the line the 4th Division. By evening the army had reached a line from Hsiatangchih across the Hualinshan mountain to the Wutaishan mountain on the main road.

The Japanese Advance

On the left the advance was opposed by Samssonoff's cavalry and horse artillery, and it was necessary for the advance guard artillery to come into action.[1] On the right the 5th Division occupied Tangchih, but were obliged to again evacuate that place.

For the 24th Oku issued orders for the 5th Division to attack the Tapingling Pass, the 3rd Division

[1] B. O. R., i. 97.

to advance on their left as far as a hill north of Shanhsitou. Connecting with the left of the 3rd, the 6th Division was to attack the hill north of Kanchiatun, taking particular care to protect its left front. The 4th Division and one regiment of artillery from the Artillery Brigade was to occupy Wutaishan to protect the left flank of the army, and " no advance was to be made therefrom till it was observed that the general attack elsewhere was succeeding."

The Artillery Brigade (less one regiment) was to take up a position on the Hualinshan and to open fire against Wangmatai, and also against the hill west of the Tapingling Pass.

The cavalry brigade was to cover the left.

The reserve (one regiment each, 3rd and 6th Divisions) was to be at Tulaopotien.

The Battle of Tashichiao

At 5.30 A.M. in the morning on the 24th the first Japanese guns opened fire, and were answered by the fire of the concealed guns of the I. Siberian Corps. Gradually the Japanese brought no less than thirteen batteries, or seventy-eight guns, into action against the I. Siberian Corps, but were unable to silence the Russian guns. About 9 A.M. the infantry of the 6th Division advanced, but not with any determination, and as a result Stakelberg was able to keep his infantry sheltered and did not occupy the trenches; nevertheless he thought that the main attack was to be pressed against his corps, and counselled Zarubaieff to retreat. His advice was ignored. When the 6th Division had reached Kanchiatun the 4th Division advanced, though temporarily checked by enfilade fire from the horse artillery with Kossakowski, and dismounted fire action of the Cossacks. The 4th Division occupied a line from Liupaitassu to Niuchiatun, and seventy-two more guns were brought into action. The result of this fighting was that two infantry divisions supported by 144 guns failed to defeat twenty-four weak battalions supported by sixty-four guns. This result was due entirely to the artillery; and, further, three of the eight Russian batteries were able to assist the battle of the IV. Siberian Corps on the left.

Meanwhile on the right the 5th Japanese Division had advanced over very difficult ground, and pushed back the Russian advanced troops on to the main line. The Japanese were able to bring seventy-two guns into action on this flank, but the superior metal of the Russian pieces enabled them to check the Japanese infantry. A desperate assault by the firing line of the 3rd Division was thrown back by a determined local counter-attack with the bayonet. Gradually the reserves on both sides were drawn into the fight; but the Japanese could make no progress, and as Oku had only held two regiments in his reserve, and had utilised one to support the left, he was unable to further reinforce his right, without denuding himself of the means of repulsing a counter-attack.

About midday Zarubaieff had instructed General Shileiko, who commanded the left, to communicate with Mischenko, with a view to making a counter-attack. An attempt was made to advance, a battalion moving in the direction of Yangtsaokou, but the movement met resistance and came to nothing, and, as about this time the Japanese 5th Division gained a little ground, the idea of a counter-attack was given up.

As the sun set the artillery fire broke out again afresh, and in the dusk repeated attacks were made by parties of the Japanese infantry. Finally, about 10 P.M., when the moon rose,[1] the 5th Division attacked and reached the first line of trenches. There was bloody hand-to-hand fighting in the dark, but the Japanese got no farther at the moment..

Meanwhile Zarubaieff, who had learnt that the artillery ammunition was very short, and had now only six battalions of his reserve left, had decided to retreat. This he did without loss, and about 3 A.M. the 5th Division occupied the main line of trenches on the Tapingling Pass, which was found held only by a rearguard.

[1] B. O. R., i. 101.

The Russians retired on Haicheng, burning their stores at Tashichiao. The Japanese followed, but gave up the pursuit three or four miles north of Tashichiao.

Occupation of Yinkou   On the 26th Yinkou was occupied, the Russian detachment there retiring on Niuchuang.

The losses on either side were not heavy: Russians, 620;[1] Japanese, 1044.

The capture of Tashichiao was strategically of the greatest importance, for it is the junction of the railway from Yinkou, and thus opened a valuable line of communications to the Japanese. The engagement was typical of the Russian defensive methods. There was no reason for the Russians to retire.

Comments

"The frontal attack of the Japanese 2nd Army supported by 252 guns had made but little impression upon the Russian artillery, which at the highest estimate fell short of half that number of pieces. The skilful use of ground by the Russians kept the positions of their guns hidden from the more numerous artillery of the Japanese, who, in order to support the infantry attack, and to counteract the longer-ranging weapons of their adversaries, were forced to make frequent changes of position, at the cost of casualties in men and horses. The

[1] G. S., ii. p. 63, places Russian losses at 2000 (about).

Russian army had, indeed, much cause for satisfaction at the day's fighting. For fifteen hours it had withstood the assaults of its formidable, and hitherto successful, opponents; while the brunt of the attack had been borne by a reserve division. Yet all the self-sacrifice and courage of the troops were wasted, and the battle was decided, as many other battles have been, by events beyond the immediate scene of action, and by the character of the rival generals; for while the Japanese prepared to renew the attack, General Zarubaieff retired."[1] The student of history will at once remember how Napoleon stood fast after the drawn battle of Eylau while Bennigsen retired. In that case, however, Napoleon's marshals urged retreat, Bennigsen's generals begged him to stand. It should also be noticed, as bearing on the weakness of the Russian strategical conceptions, that by the middle of July Kuropatkin had at Haicheng and Hsimucheng the following troops:

> 1st Brigade 2nd Sib. Inf. Division (IV. Corps)
> 5th E. S. R. Division
> 35th Infantry Division
> 2nd Brigade 31st Inf. Division

At this time the only troops threatening Hsimucheng was the 10th Division, which had recently captured the Fenshuiling Pass. Thus Kuropatkin

[1] G. S., ii. 62.

could have easily placed three strong brigades, if not four, at Zarubaieff's disposal for a great counter-stroke.

The peculiar relations of the subordinate generals to Zarubaieff and to one another are of great interest. That Stakelberg should have suggested retreat when his infantry had not occupied their trenches is singular; but the negotiations which resulted in the abortive counter-attack against the 5th Division were still more remarkable. General Shileiko had first to "arrange" the co-operation of Mischenko. To this he obtained that general's "consent." However, when he sought to obtain the assistance of the troops on his right under General Kossovitch, he was met with a blank refusal.[1]

A bold offensive movement on this flank might have resulted in driving back the 5th Division. It would however, in all probability, have only had a temporary success. In this connection it is to be noted that co-operation between the various Russian leaders was most loyal during the defence.[2]

The effect of the withdrawal on the moral of the Russian troops was bad, as is witnessed by Herr von Schwartz, a German war correspondent. The interest of the engagement hinges principally on the action of the artillery. So impressed had Stakelberg been by the results of the fire of the

[1] R. M. G. (1907), vol. ii. p. 162. [2] G. S., ii. p. 60.

concealed Japanese guns at Telissu, that he placed all his batteries under cover. The original positions constructed had been in the open, and the empty pits were shelled by the Japanese. The only battery that suffered severely was the 4th of the 1st East Siberian Rifle Division, which changed position to a spot whence its flashes were visible.[1] The artillery of the IV. Siberian Corps was not quite so well concealed, and some of its batteries suffered heavily.

With regard to the Japanese dispositions, it cannot be said that they were skilful. "Combined Training" points out that the power of the modern arms confers increased facility for manœuvre on the assailant, by enabling him to establish an impenetrable screen and manœuvre at ease behind it. The Japanese possessed undoubted superiority of manœuvre over the Russians. Their left flank in a manœuvre by the left would be secured by the fleet, their right in a manœuvre through the mountains by the 10th Division. Yet Oku made a pure frontal attack on a carefully-prepared position.

Towards the end of July, as the Japanese did not follow up their success at Tashichiao, and as

[1] Article by Colonel Pachenkoin *The Russian Artillery Journal.*

Russian Dispositions the situation of the 12th Division appeared to be isolated, while at the same time it threatened the Russian line of retreat, Kuropatkin, on the 27th July, ordered the X. Corps to collect at Anping and cover the left of the army, with the intention of initiating an offensive movement against the Japanese right. About the 30th July, then, the Russian troops were distributed generally as follows:—

> Haicheng: with detachment at Niuchuang: I. and IV. Siberian Corps
> Hsimucheng: II. Siberian Corps
> Tawan: East Detachment (III. Siberian Corps)
> Yushuling: X. Corps
> Arriving at Liaoyang: XVII. Corps
> Covering the left: Rennenkampf's Cossack Division
> Covering the south front: Samssonoff and Mischenko's Cavalry Brigades

Japanese Dispositions Oyama now issued orders for the advance of the 1st and 4th Armies, and this led to a series of engagements.

On the 17th July General Baron Nodzu had arrived at Hsiuyen and assumed command of the **4th Army** 4th Army, now consisting of the 10th Division and a reserve brigade. On the 22nd the "mixed" Guards brigade marched to rejoin the 1st Army, and on the same day, under orders from headquarters, to assist the advance of the 2nd Army, Nodzu moved his troops in several columns up to the advanced troops, and by the 24th was on a line some ten miles south of Hsimucheng. The right column had some severe fighting before it came into line.

Advancing thence, by the 28th the force had reached a line of high ground east of Yanglahuo to Changchiaputzu, main body at Lamufang, reserve at Yanglahuo.

The 5th Division (right of the 2nd Army) was about five miles north of Tangchih, and in touch with the left of the 10th Division. At 10.30 P.M. on the 28th Nodzu received instructions from headquarters to capture Hsimucheng, and the 5th Division was placed under his orders, and from now on belonged to the 4th Army.

Since the capture of the Fenshuiling and the retreat of General Lewetsam to Hsimucheng at the end of June, the headquarters of the II. Siberian Corps (Zassulich) had been established there. The troops belonging to the corps assembled at Hsimucheng were (it is believed):

Russian Disposition

  5th East Siberian Rifle Division, complete
  2nd Brigade 31st Infantry Division
  1st Brigade 2nd East Siberian Infantry Division
  2 regiments of Cossacks
  8 batteries

A fortified position had, as usual, been prepared with care. The main position was occupied by two regiments, 5th East Siberian Rifle Division, with one in reserve; while the right was held by the 1st Brigade 2nd East Siberian Infantry Division. The 2nd Brigade 31st Infantry Division formed the General Reserve. General Mischenko was in touch to the westward.

The position extended some distance to the west of Hsimucheng. The left rested on a considerable hill north of the village of Hungyaoling, and stretched outwards convexive to the Japanese along a ridge to the village of Sanchiaoshan. Westward of this a considerable hill was held as the right of the position.[1]

The Position

This position had a frontage of nearly seven and a half miles, an immense extension for twenty-six battalions. The right, where the country is very rough and mountainous, was covered by Mischenko.

In spite of the difficulty of the country in front of his left, Nodzu decided to send the 5th Division against the enemy's right and rear, while the 10th Division attacked in front, and a column consisting of the bulk of the 10th Reserve Brigade turned the Russian left.

Japanese Plan of Attack

For the 30th the troops were therefore ordered to reach the following positions:—10th Reserve Brigade and 10th Division, a line Tafanghsin, Shanchengtzu, hill north of Hsiapachoukou; 5th Division, advanced troops, hill south-east Kuchia-

[1] K. E., 41, 42, 49.

putzu - Yunglaoshah - Wangchiaputzu; main body, Houshihlakou.

There was a gap of about five miles between the left of the 10th and the right of the 5th division, and special arrangements were made for intercommunication.

The troops reached the places assigned for them on the 30th; the 10th Division and 10th Reserve Brigade being in three columns, the 5th Division also in three columns.

At dawn on the 31st the 10th Division attacked and drove in the Russian advanced troops from the hills south of Hsimucheng and west of Tapingling, but failed to occupy the main position at that time.

The Attack

Meanwhile, on the left the 5th Division advanced at midnight, and pushing steadily forward, by 10 A.M. had occupied, after severe fighting, the hills north and west of Hangchiaputzu; here they got in touch with a mixed brigade of the 3rd Division sent out from the 2nd Army to co-operate. From this point some of their artillery could join in the attack of the Russian main position, and destroyed a battery of the 31st Infantry Division which had reinforced the Russian right.

About 11.30 A.M. a very determined assault by the 10th Division succeeded, and the hill was occupied. While this was taking place, Kawamura had sent the divisional reserve to reinforce his left, but they came under the fire of the Russian batteries posted on a saddle north of Hangchiaputzu, and were forced to halt, the two batteries coming into action.

Hearing that the 5th Division had taken the hill on the Russian right, Nodzu thought that the Russians would retire, and despatched the General Reserve (one regiment) via Tafanghsin against the Russian left. The divisional reserve of the 10th Division also again attempted to advance. The Russians, however, had no intention of retreating, and the reserves having been brought up, Zassulich ordered a counter-attack to be made on the captured position west of Hsimucheng. After repeated assaults, which gained some small success at first, the attack was repulsed by the Japanese, and the I. Siberian Corps withdrew, under orders from Kuropatkin, received about 11 P.M.,[1] to Haicheng, and thence early in August to Anshanchan.

The losses in the engagement were: Russians, 1550; Japanese, 836.

On the 1st August the 4th Army continued its advance, on finding that the Russians had vacated their positions. The advance was continued on the 2nd by the 2nd Army as well as the 4th. On the 4th August Haicheng was occupied.

Further Movements

[1] K. E., 41, 42, 52.

Reverting to the movements on the eastern front, as a result of the engagements of the 17th and 19th July the Japanese 1st Army held a line from west of Chiaotou over the Motienling, along the line of passes to the Sandoling Pass,[1] held by the left of the Guard division. The Guard Reserve Brigade was coming up in rear of the right, though exactly where it was is not apparent. One regiment at any rate had been up for some time,[2] for at Aiyangcheng on the 22nd June a major of a reserve regiment was killed.

1st Army

It will be recalled that in front of Kuroki had stood: the Eastern Detachment commanded by Count Keller, the 9th Division (X. Corps) commanded by Herschelman, and Rennenkampf's Cossack Division (commanded at present by General Ljubavin), about nineteen squadrons and twelve guns.

Russians

The capture of Chiaotou startled Kuropatkin, and on the 21st July he ordered General Sluchevski, the commander of the X. Corps, to collect his corps, to which was added the Kuban and Argansk Cossack Regiments, and a mountain battery, at Anping. The 2nd Brigade of the 31st Division, with a group of artillery, remained with the II. Siberian Corps.

The 2nd Brigade of the 9th Division formed a screen, and by the 24th July the corps was con-

---

[1] Not on Map.   [2] B. O. R., i. 141.

centrated. Kuropatkin proceeded to Anping in person. "Six regiments of cavalry and very nearly two whole divisions of infantry under the commander-in-chief in person were now massed against the Japanese right; but it was decided that no attack could be delivered, as the information about the enemy was not sufficiently definite. In this way four valuable days were wasted."[1] Meanwhile, the battle of Tashichiao and Zarubaieff's retreat caused Kuropatkin to return to Liaoyang, leaving to Sluchevski the prosecution of the offensive movement against the isolated 12th Japanese Division. Sluchevski proposed to advance systematically against the Japanese right at Chiaotou, fortifying his position each day as he advanced. He divided his corps into:—Advanced guard, two regiments, one squadron, two batteries, which advanced to the Yushuling Pass, occupying the ridge of Hsishan and driving back the Japanese posts. Main body, five squadrons, seven battalions, five batteries field, five guns mountain artillery, placed east of the village of Laoguanlin; the artillery at Tundiapu. Right flank guard, one and a half squadrons, two regiments, two battalions, one battery, two mountain guns, placed on the Pienling Pass to keep open communication with the East Detachment. The Japanese posts here also fell back

[1] O. S., ii. 109.

without fighting. Left flank guard, six squadrons, one battalion, sent to the northward, to connect with the brigade of Cossacks near Penhsihu.

The troops were in these positions on the 29th, ready to advance. On the 30th some changes in the artillery distribution had to be made,[1] and so the corps remained halted and began to strengthen its entrenchments; thus the great systematic forward movement did not continue.

Facing the Japanese Guard and 2nd Division, the East Detachment now consisted of: the 3rd and 6th East Siberian Rifle Divisions, one regiment of Cossacks, and a mountain battery; a total of three squadrons, twenty-four battalions, and sixty-eight guns.[2]

The position occupied by Count Keller formed a rough semicircle of which the centre was the Yangtzuling Pass, which the 2nd and Guard Divisions must use for their further advance. From the Pass runs a small stream which joins the Lan river at Tawan. The heights which form the gully in which this stream runs were occupied by the Russians, and at the point where the gully merges into the main valley these heights are only some 300 yards apart. At this point the Russian position presented a sharp salient beneath which there was an area of dead ground distinctly favourable

[1] K. E., 41, 42, 67.   [2] G. S., ii. p. 161.

to the attack. Nevertheless the heights themselves are so rugged and broken that they can only be scaled with the utmost difficulty : at one point upon which a Russian battery was placed the ground dropped in a sheer precipiece of eighty feet into the bed of the river. But before this dead ground could be reached the Japanese must cross the valley of the Lan river, about 800 yards in width. All the valleys leading into this main valley from the Japanese position were commanded by the Russian artillery.

South of the main position a spur which guards the road from Chuchiaputzu was held by a regiment, while in rear of the right the 22nd East Siberian Rifle Regiment formed a refused flank to guard against a turning movement.

The whole position was prepared for defence with the utmost care, with two exceptions, the crops in the Lan river valley were left standing, and the villages, though held, were not prepared for defence.[1]

Only twenty-eight field and the four mountain guns were placed in position and took part in the action.[2]

It is not yet clear how the troops were distributed, but it would seem that the 6th East Siberian Rifle

[1] G. S., ii. 112.
[2] G. S., ii. 161 (footnote).

Division occupied the position and the whole 3rd East Siberian Rifle Division were held in reserve.[1]

General Kuroki decided to take the offensive along the whole line on the 31st July, and for this purpose divided his army as follows:—For the attack on the X. Corps, he detailed the 12th Division, with five reserve (Kobi) battalions,[2] and a detachment of four battalions from the 2nd Division; for the attack on the East Detachment (or III. Siberian Corps, as it was afterwards called) were detailed the Guard and 2nd Divisions (less four battalions).

Japanese Plan of Attack

Thus the battle divided itself naturally into two almost totally distinct engagements, for between the right of the X. and left of the III. Siberian Corps was an almost unoccupied space of about four miles in an air line, filled with pathless and rugged hills.

For the attack on the East Detachment Kuroki decided to hold the enemy in front and turn his right.

The Action on the Yushuling Pass

General Nishi, commanding the 2nd Division, distributed his force for the holding attack, to be ready at daybreak, as follows:—Three battalions and four batteries to be north of Chinchiaputzu; two battalions and two batteries south of the same place; one and a half

[1] G. S., ii. 116.
[2] G. S., ii. 111.

battalions to form the reserve,[1] east of Chinchiaputzu; the cavalry regiment and one and a half battalions to cover the right flank and reconnoitre in the valley of the Lan river.

The guards, who were to attack and outflank the Russian right, were divided into four columns, which may be called G1, G2, G3, and G4, in order from the right, and were formed as follows:—

> G1, 1 troop, 3 battalions, 3 batteries, to march via the Hsinkailing Pass to Makoumentzu.
> G2, half troop, 2 battalions, 2 batteries, to march via the Lanholin Pass by a road made practicable the previous afternoon (30th) and cross the valley near Shuitayangtzu.
> G3, 2 troops, 3 battalions, one mountain battery (from 12th Division, in exchange for a field battery), to march via the Papanling Pass.
> G4, 2 and a half troops, three battalions (less 1 company), 1 battery, to march via Mayaputzu.

The remainder of the cavalry, one and a quarter squadrons, were to go to Mayaputzu and cover the left.

Divisional headquarters were with the reserve, one battalion, which was to follow G3.[2]

Intercommunication between the columns was to be maintained by the field telephone.

This distribution was intended to secure that G1 and G2, both of which were commanded by General

[1] K. E., 41, 42, 73. [2] B. O. R., i. 191.

Asada, were to attack the right of the Russian line, while G3 outflanked and attacked the right flank, and G4, passing the right, took the line in rear.

On the night of the 30th the divisions marched by the light of the moon, and by daybreak on the 31st, a blazing hot day, the troops had reached the positions indicated on Map XI.

G1 brought nine guns into action about 6 A.M., but could not find a position for the remaining nine. About midday the infantry advanced towards the south-west, but were unable to get close to the Russian trenches.

Action of the Guards

G2 had great difficulties on the march, but managed to get its guns into action about 7.50 A.M.[1] The Russians, however, silenced these batteries, which ceased firing about 8.20 A.M. The ground was very difficult, and the guns had to come into action one by one as available.

About 9 A.M. the infantry advanced to the attack, covered by the *kaoliang* until they had to cross the bed of the Lan river, 250 yards wide.[2] They cleared the village of Shuitayangtzu, and about 12.30 P.M. reached a ridge, from which, however, they were unable to advance across the 250 yards or so separating them from the Russian trenches, chiefly on account of enfilade fire from the right.

G3 brought its battery into action soon after

[1] B. O. R., i. 195.   [2] S. O. M. Z. (1906), vol. i. 432.

daybreak, and sent the infantry forward. They advanced, covered by the *kaoliang*, against Kachiaputzu and Hanchiaputzu. By 1 P.M. they were within a few hundred yards of the Russian lines, but they did not get farther all day.

G4, after a long and tiring march, reached the position shown in the sketch about 1 P.M. Here they halted, not knowing anything about the other columns. Intercommunication by field telephone proved quite useless, and it was impossible for the different columns to know what was happening elsewhere.

At 9.5 A.M. four batteries of the 2nd Division came into action, and continued bombarding the Russian trenches for some time. Later the other three batteries came into action. An artillery duel continued till about 10 A.M., during which the Japanese suffered severely.

2nd Division

About noon the Japanese reopened fire on the Russian artillery positions, and about 2 P.M. another duel began.

At 3.30 P.M., as the Guards' advance had stopped, Kuroki decided to send the 2nd Division infantry forward to the attack, and the columns G1 and G2 were ordered to co-operate. The divisional reserve was sent into the fight to join G2, but without effect. A Russian counter-attack through the scrub on G2, from the spur which they held in such close proximity, was beaten back.[1]

The attack of the 2nd Division was the last resort, and the whole available force (six battalions) took part in it. It should be remembered that at this time the result of the action of his 12th Division against the X. Corps was not known to Kuroki.

Pushing steadily forward under a hail of shrapnel, the advance was hardly opposed by the Russian infantry, who were withdrawing. Count Keller, who is described by Freiherr von Tettau as a "knightly spirit," had died a soldier's death amongst his men, having been struck down with thirty-six wounds from a shrapnel shell which burst close to him. His death took the heart out of the Russian defence, and his successor decided to withdraw, though there was no necessity whatever to retreat.

By 5.30 P.M. the Japanese infantry had occupied the Russian trenches.

The Actions at Yushulintzu and Pienling

Returning to the battle of the 12th Division and X. Corps, the Russian position at Yushulintzu was on the Hsishan ridge. This ridge forms the southern side of the Hsi river valley, a flat stretch of about 2500 yards wide and well cultivated. The Hsishan ridge is

[1] S. O. M. Z. (1906), vol. i. 432.

dominated from the north of the valley, by a mountain called by the Japanese Makurayama, connected to the northern wall of mountains by a col. Makurayama was occupied by the 122nd Infantry Regiment, and on the Hsishan were placed two batteries and the 121st Regiment. The batteries had great difficulty in reaching their station owing to the ground. They were not on one position, but dispersed in three groups.[1] The front of the 121st Regiment was over 4000 yards.[2] The right flank detachment had placed its infantry in position on the Pienling Pass, but its artillery had been left at Lipiyu.

Neither of the positions on the Yushuling and Pienling passes were so carefully prepared as was Count Keller's position on the Yangtzuling Pass.[3]

After the battle of the 19th July General Inouye had occupied the ridge of Chiaotou. Five miles farther west is the Hsishan ridge.

"At first sight it would appear that there were but two courses open, either to remain on the Chiaotou ridge or to occupy the Hsishan ridge. But General Inouye thought otherwise, and probably with good reason."[4] The Hsishan ridge was dominated by heights further west; and so General

[1] F. v. T., i. p. 211.   [2] K. E., 41, 42, p. 68.
[3] It should be remembered that Ljubavin, with 5 battalions, 21 squadrons, 16 guns, was at Penhsihu.
[4] G. S., ii. 111.

Inouye preferred to advance near to the eastern foot of the ridge, and there to solidly entrench himself and deliberately allow the Russians to occupy the Hsishan ridge, where Inouye considered that from his position he could attack them with every prospect of success. This proceeding was peculiar, and merits particular attention.[1]

Japanese Plan of Attack   To attack the Russians General Inouye divided his force into four portions:—

Right column, to attack the Yushuling position:

1 brigade (6 battalions), 5 batteries

Left column, to attack the Pienling position:

1 squadron, 1 brigade (less 1 battalion), 1 battery

This column was to be assisted by four battalions, 2nd Division.

Right flank guard, in the direction of Penhsihu:

3 squadrons, 1 battery
5 battalions Guard Reserve Brigade[2]

Reserve:

1 battalion, 1 battalion engineers (less detachments)

The idea was to seize Makurayama and Pienling first. The whole force could then attack the Hsishan ridge.

It should be remembered that the X. Corps was formed of infantry regiments of four battalions each, not rifle regiments of three battalions. It was short of one Brigade. The

The X. Corps

[1] G. S., ii. 112.   [2] G. S., ii. p. 118.

corps had a balloon, which did not render much service.

During the night of 30th-31st a position for two batteries was dug on the left of the line of Japanese entrenchments. extending across the Hsi river valley, about 100 yards behind the crest of a slight slope.[1]

Japanese Attack

At 4 A.M. the right column started for the attack of Makurayama, two battalions attacking in front, three battalions moving along the hills to turn the Russian right.

The right attack succeeded in surprising the piquet on the col joining Makurayama to the main ridge, and, dashing forward, reached the crest before the Russians and opened fire on their camp. The Russians, hastily falling in, endeavoured to recover the hill; the commander of the 2nd battalion, Colonel Lipovan, took his battalion forward with the bayonet on his own initiative.[2] Meanwhile, the second Japanese battalion had succeeded in reaching, unobserved, the dead ground at the foot of the hill, and attacked the Russians who were engaged with the enemy on the col. At 7.7 A.M.[3] the Japanese guns opened fire, and by 8.30 A.M. Makurayama was entirely in the hands of the Japanese infantry, the 122nd Regiment retreating to a ridge about a mile west of Makurayama, General

[1] B. O. R., i. p. 212.   [2] F. v. T., i. p. 214.   [3] B. O. R., i. 216.

Grekoff, who commanded the Russian left flank guard, sent assistance, in the shape of two sotnias and two mounted scout detachments. Three companies were sent over from the right flank, and about 10 A.M. a battalion of the 33rd Regiment came up into the firing line, while a battalion of the 34th Regiment formed up in reserve behind the left flank.

The very inferior Japanese infantry under an enfilade fire from Hsishan could not advance, nor could they occupy the bare crest of Makurayama. About 9.30 A.M. a fierce counter-attack was delivered, but was repulsed. No more Russian batteries were brought up, though the Japanese fire was very accurate, and prevented the few Russian guns from assisting their infantry.[1]

The Japanese artillery advanced about 7 A.M. to a covered position about 3100 yards from the main Russian position, but only nineteen guns were able to find space to come into action.[2]

Meanwhile, the three batteries on the left had advanced and occupied the hill above Liensha. Seeing that a further advance was difficult, they awaited the action of the left column, entrenching themselves on the edge of a *kaoliang* field.

Towards noon the firing died away.

The left column marched at 5.30 A.M., and occu-

[1] F. v. T., i. 219.   [2] B. O. R., i. 216.

pied East Pienling at 7 A.M. almost without resistance. The attack on the main position at West Pienling proved difficult, although the Russians were without artillery. At 8 A.M. the Japanese battery opened fire, but found the Russian infantry difficult to locate. The Russian right now endeavoured to envelop the Japanese left. The Japanese artillery, however, succeeded in finding the Russian infantry in a sunken road, and a few men (said to be a party of seven [1]) worked round and enfiladed the Russian left. A battalion was sent up to reinforce the Russian left, but the Japanese, seeing their chance, dashed forward and seized a crest, from which they were able to fire on the reinforcements. The whole of the troops on the Russian left were then obliged to retire over a narrow gully, in which they suffered heavy losses.

Left Column

About 11 A.M. the entire Russian line commenced to retreat into the valley west of the position. At this moment General Okasaki, with four battalions of the 2nd Division, arrived on the flank of the Russian line of retreat. A straggling engagement ensued. The Japanese pushed on over the very difficult ground in pursuit, but at every point of vantage the Russians turned to bay. About 3 P.M. a Russian battery near Lipiyu opened fire on the pursuers, who thereupon halted.

[1] I. H., vol. i. 355.

General Sluchevski, on hearing of the engagement at Pienling, sent forward two battalions from the reserve, and also reinforced the troops on Hsishan. The retreating troops from Pienling, which had rallied beyond Lipiyu, were ordered to advance, but did not do so.

About the same time Grekoff reported the advance of infantry and artillery against the left. It is not clear what these troops were.

About 3 P.M. a further attempt to advance was made by the Japanese, and again about 7 P.M. a furious cannonade preluded an attempt to advance, but both attempts failed.

As the right flank of the corps was turned, Sluchevski gave orders in the night of 31st-1st to retreat. The retreat took place successfully and in perfect order. A rearguard was placed on the Laguling Pass, with one battalion at Lipiyu. The Japanese attacked this rearguard about 5 A.M. on the 1st, but it withdrew skilfully. The corps retired to a position in front of Anping.

The losses on either side were: Japanese, 989, Russians, 2459, of whom only 391 belonged to the East Detachment.

Comments
The three engagements of the 31st placed Oyama's troops in a much more satisfactory position strategically. The 2nd and 4th Armies, forming a mass of some 80,000 to 90,000 men, were now concentrated about Hai-

cheng, within three marches of Liaoyang, while Kuroki, with a force of some 50,000, stood at a distance of only twenty miles from that town. The advantage of the interior lines was, therefore, to some extent lost to Kuropatkin.

In order to place his troops in closer communication, Oyama could have either moved the 1st Army to its left or else done as he did and order it to advance. The latter method seemed the more satisfactory, for it did not relieve the Russians from the constant and rather paralysing effect of the threatening situation of Kuroki on their left flank. It was this threat which had induced Kuropatkin to send the X. Corps forward, and it is probable that Oyama, knowing of the movement, determined to forestall the Russians and take the offensive himself.

Possibly Oyama hoped to deal such a blow at the isolated East Detachment that the 1st Army would succeed in reaching the line of the Tang river without further opposition, and the operations of the Guard Division were undoubtedly aimed at a complete envelopment of the right of this corps.

In both battles the attack of the Japanese on the main position failed, but the Russians, following their usual practice, retired without attempting to take advantage of their tactical position.[1]

[1] I. H., i. 338.

It is noteworthy that the Russian troops on this front were three detached forces—Keller's, Sluchevski's, and Ljubavin's. The Japanese were under one command, that of Kuroki.

The failure of the various columns of the Guard to co-operate is striking. Isolation has a most paralysing effect on a battlefield, and the field telephone proved a broken reed to lean on.

The action of the X. Corps is most interesting. The Russian "position" tactics induced Sluchevski to place a force equal to one division (about 11,500 men) and two batteries on a front of nearly six miles. Thus he was weak everywhere. It is true that his left regiment allowed itself to be surprised, and we now know that only two battalions opposed it, about 2000 strong, while it mustered some 2800 rifles. When it was supported the reinforcements came up at long intervals. The whole of Sluchevski's considerable reserve was thus frittered away by being employed in driblets, not in a mass capable of decisive action. Of his eighty-eight field-guns only sixteen at Hsishan and four at Lipiyu came into action. True, the ground was bad, but Freiherr von Tettau distinctly states that more could have been brought up.

The strength of the X. Corps was about 19,000 and eighty-eight guns, it was attacked and forced to retreat by 16,000 men and some thirty guns, for the Japanese right flank guard did not come into action.

Section 107 in "Combined Training" says: "The strength of the assailant has always lain in the moral advantage conferred by the initiative, in his power of manœuvring, of hiding his movements, and of concentrating unexpectedly against some weak or ill-defended point," such, for example, as the Russian position at Pienling. The words quoted are practically those of the late Colonel Henderson. It would be hard to find a better illustration of the doctrine therein enunciated than this engagement. At the decisive point, Pienling, Inouye brought together nine battalions against four distributed over some two miles of ground. Furthermore, the concentration was quite unexpected.

By the end of July, Nogi had collected his troops at Dalny, and on the 26th he moved in six columns against the Russian position, known as the Green Hills Line. In the afternoon the artillery and a regiment of 4.72 howitzers came into action, and the Japanese infantry worked up to the foot of the Russian position. In the night of 26th-27th

Port Arthur

an attack was delivered, but failed. On the 27th the attack was resumed, and boldly pressed in spite of terrible losses. The left (sixth) column was taken in flank by the Russian cruisers.

During the night a determined attack was made on the Russian right, and it was successful. This made the whole line untenable, and the Russians withdrew on to their next line, known as the Wolf's Mountain Line.

On the 30th, while Kuroki's and Nodzu's troops were preparing to attack the last passages from the hills into the plain of Liaoyang, Nogi's troops advanced to drive the Russians from their last position outside the fortress. The position was not strong, and the foreground was covered with *kaoliang*. The left wing was turned, and the Russians retired into the fortress.

From Nanshan to Wolf's Mountain there had been over two months for the Russians to prepare

Comments
for the defence of the fortress, and under Smirnoff and Kondratenko the work was ably carried on.

General Stoessel's measures for the fights in the neighbourhood require no special comment. They evinced great lack of tactical skill on the part of most of the generals and their staffs, great endurance, gallantry, and determination on the part of the regimental officers and men.

General Situation After the engagements of the 31st July, Kuropatkin divided his army into two fronts, and distributed them as follows:—

South Front

1st Cavalry Division:
  24 squadrons
  16 guns
2nd Cavalry Division:
  24 squadrons
  12 guns
I. Siberian Corps:
  6 squadrons
  24 battalions
  1 battalion engineers
  64 guns
II. Siberian Corps:
  12 squadrons
  20 battalions
  1 battalion engineers
  86 guns
IV. Siberian Corps:
  6 squadrons
  32 battalions
  1 battalion engineers
  128 guns

East Front:

III. Corps (late East Detachment)
  6 squadrons
  24 battalions
  1 battalion engineers
  72 guns

X. Corps:
> 12 squadrons
> 32 battalions
> 1 battalion
> 1 company engineers
> 88 guns

XVII. Corps:
> 6 squadrons
> 16 battalions
> 1 battalion engineers
> 48 guns

Central Connecting Force—Lieutenant Colonel Madritoff:
> 16 squadrons
> 2 battalions
> 2 guns

Right Flank Guard:
> 9 squadrons
> 2 and a half battalions
> 4 guns

Left Flank Guard—Ljubavin:
> 19 squadrons
> 12 guns

In and around Liaoyang:
> 6 squadrons
> 2 battalions
> 1 battalion engineers

Mukden, Kirin, and Harbin:
> 8 battalions (1st Siberian Reserve Division)
> 3 squadrons

Vladivostok and Neighbourhood:

    27 squadrons
    22 battalions
    64 guns
    Fortress troops

Lines of communication troops, depôt and reserve squadrons, depôt and reserve battalions:

    About 24 battalions
    73 squadrons
    240 guns

In Transport, east of Lake Baikal:

    1st Brigade 35th Division, XVII. Corps
    V. Siberian Corps
    Drafts

Distribution The troops in front of Liaoyang were distributed as follows:—

South Front (at present commanded by Kuropatkin in person, later by Zarubaieff)—I., II., and IV. Siberian Army Corps, in the position at Anshanchan, with advanced posts to the south towards Haicheng and south-west in the hills.

East Front (General Bilderling)—III. Siberian Corps at Langtzushan, X. Corps at Anping. The left rested on the Taitse river; detachments occupied the positions along the line of passes leading into the valley of the Tang river from the east. XVII. Corps in General Reserve near Liaoyang.

In the gap between the two fronts from Kutsantzu to Tanghsinpu stood General Madritoff with his detachment.[1]

To cover the right flank a detachment was placed in the valley of the Liao River, consisting of :

9 squadrons, 2 and a half battalions, four guns.

To cover the left, on the north bank of the Taitsehò, about Penhsihu, was placed General Ljubavin.

The Japanese were distributed as follows:—

1st Army—Kuroki (Headquarters Tientsuitien): 12th, 2nd, Guard Divisions in the order named on the western side of the Lan River. Guards "mixed" reserve brigade at Chiaotou.

4th Army—Nodzu: Part of the 10th Reserve Brigade and the 10th Division near Feishun; 5th Division on their left. Right flank guard at Tieshantun, part 10th Reserve Brigade in reserve at Hsimucheng.

2nd Army—Oku: 3rd, 5th, 4th Divisions at Haicheng. In transport on the railway, 11th Reserve Brigade.[2]

The lines of communication are still uncertain.

Those of the 1st Army ran back on Antung, but troops of reserve formations were stationed along the Saimachi road. Probably some supplies came up from Shuitien along this road to the 12th Division.

The 4th Army's communications ran back to

[1] But see G. S., ii. p. 121, in which the distribution is slightly different.
[2] K. E., 41, 42, 78.

Takushan, but they certainly received some supplies from the railway.

The 2nd Army was based partly on Yinkou and partly on Talienwan.

The armies remained substantially in these positions until 22nd August.

CHAPTER VI

A Comment on the Strategy of the Belligerents up to the end of July—Some Notes on the Tactics of both Sides

IN Chapter I. the probable course of action of both belligerents was considered, on the basis of the respective positions at the outbreak of war. Certain unexpected things, however, happened, as is always the case in war. Firstly, Japan gained the command of the sea within two days of the outbreak of hostilities, and not only was this command never seriously challenged during the first year of war, but the transport of troops, etc., to the mainland was almost as safe for Japan as if the Russian navy had not existed. The next unexpected event was that the Russian troops on the Yalu allowed themselves to be drawn into a serious engagement against a many-times superior enemy, with the inevitable result.

General Remarks

The proceedings of the Japanese were marked throughout by the greatest prudence and forethought. Still, no prudence could avoid the difficulties of the march through Korea, though, in view of

Japanese Methodical Procedure

the very weak force opposing the advance, it is not quite clear why the guards and the 2nd Division were landed at Chinampo, and not conveyed to one of the ports further north, when the harbours of Rikaho, Boto, Quiempo, etc., became ice-free. It would seem that had this been done the advance to Wiju would have been less difficult, and therefore the passage of the Yalu accomplished earlier.

Arrived at Wiju, Kuroki took a very long time (ten days) to reconnoitre the country and decide on his line of action. The reasons assigned for this are usually said to be: firstly, extreme caution, and, secondly, the necessity to collect supplies. The former reason appears the more probable, for a passage of the Yalu would have at once made Antung available as a sea base, where supplies could have been landed with great ease and despatch.

However that may be, Kuroki as soon as possible after the passage of the river advanced to Fenghuangcheng. This point is a junction of roads from Port Arthur, Kaiping, and Haicheng via Hsiuyen, from Liaoyang via Langtzushan, and from Mukden via Saimachi and Penhsihu.

Kuroki's Move to Fenghuangcheng

Placed in such a position, at a distance of only some six marches from Liaoyang and eight from

Kaiping, the 1st Army was situated within striking distance of the line of advance southward of a Russian force from Liaoyang towards Takushan or Pitzuwo.

The Japanese seem to have considered that, until Kuroki was thus established it was unsafe to land an army in the Liaotung peninsula itself. This brings us to a very debatable point, and one that has been much discussed. It has been argued that with the resources at the disposal of the Japanese, it would have been perfectly practicable to land in the Liaotung peninsula at least a month earlier than was actually done, and that in this way Port Arthur could have been blockaded before full preparations for the defence could have been made. This seems to be one of these cases in which it is difficult to judge after the event. We now know that such a move would have been quite safe, but in April 1904 it could hardly be said that the Russian fleet was no longer "a fleet in being." During this month repeated efforts were made by the Japanese to block the entrance to Port Arthur, and it is significant that it was not until this was supposed to have been successfully accomplished, that the 2nd Army sailed. Was the army of Oku awaiting the result of the battle of the Yalu, or only

Reasons for Delay in landing a second Army

the result of the attempt to safely bottle up the Russian fleet? It is evident that the Yalu position could be made untenable for the Russians by a landing near Takushan, and no doubt Oku's army was held in readiness for eventualities, either to assist Kuroki, or definitely to cut off Port Arthur.

After landing his army near Pitzuwo, Oku advanced south as rapidly as possible against General Stoessel, cut off the fortress from the outside world, drove in the advanced troops, and, having established a force to cover Dalny, the base for the siege operations, he concentrated about Pulantien and northward a force of three divisions and a cavalry brigade. Here he was delayed twelve days arranging for transport, and it cannot be said that the time was long.

The 2nd Army lands: Port Arthur blockaded

Meanwhile Kuroki was establishing a line of tramway from Antung to Fenghuangcheng, and pushing out troops to the north-eastward to threaten the Mukden road. The result of these manœuvres on the east front was to induce the Russian commander to make a detachment from his main army, amounting roughly to one cavalry division and one army corps, from a total of not much more than two cavalry divisions and three army corps. Just before the battle of Nanshan the 10th Division

Action of the East Front retains a large Russian Force

commenced landing near Takushan, and this force retained a further Russian force of a cavalry brigade and an infantry brigade. Thus Oku had to face only one cavalry brigade and two weak army corps.

As soon as possible after landing, the 10th Division, supported by half the Guard division lent by the 1st Army, advanced to Hsiuyen, an important junction of roads, and on the 12th June Oku also advanced with the 2nd Army and defeated a Russian force consisting of rather more than half Kuropatkin's disposable troops. He was soon reinforced by the 6th Division.

Thus in the middle of June we find the Japanese field army disposed in three principal groups: about 23,000 at Fenghuangcheng, with a flank guard of 7000 at Aiyangcheng, 18,000 at Hsiuyen, and 55,000 at Telissu. There were still disposable in Japan two active divisions (7th and 8th) and a cavalry brigade. The siege of Port Arthur was being prosecuted by three active divisions. The reserve formations had not yet been employed in active operations, except a battalion or two of the guards reserve brigade near Aiyangcheng.

Disposition of Japanese after the Battle of Telissu

Of these three groups the eastern was approximately six marches from Liaoyang and the others about nine marches distant. Each group was separated by about three marches from one another.

Up to this time the Japanese had had two lucky windfalls in the shape of the battles of the Yalu and Telissu.

In spite of the transport difficulties Oku was able to slowly continue his advance, thus uncovering the right of the Russian line along the main mountain chain. On the 26th June Kawamura and Kuroki, having collected supplies and arranged for transport, simultaneously advanced against the main ridge of the Fenshuiling mountains, turning the flanks of the carefully-prepared Russian positions and occupying the passes almost without opposition.

The Japanese occupy the Crests of Chienshan Mountains

Immediately after this followed the occupation of Kaiping by the 2nd Army.

In these positions the 2nd and 4th Armies were placed in close communication at about five marches from Liaoyang, and numbered in all some 80,000 men. The eastern group, numbering about 48,000, was about three marches from Liaoyang, but separated from it by difficult country.

During almost the whole of July the armies remained in these positions, with the exception that Kuroki, taking advantage of a Russian reverse on the 18th, brought up his right to Chiaotou on the 19th.

The long delay of nearly a month in these positions has caused much discussion. The roads, or

Causes for the Halt in July tracks, over which the supplies had to be brought were extraordinarily difficult, and the means of transport very inadequate. It is true that the army with which Lord Roberts occupied Bloemfontein was considerably smaller than the force under Kuroki, and that the force was obliged to make a very long halt at that place, and yet that army was supplied by a railway. Still, it cannot be said that the situations are really in any way parallel, for Lord Roberts' chief difficulties were to replace the loss of horse-flesh and draught animals and to guard his lines of communication, which were very long. None of these difficulties affected the Japanese. It would appear, therefore, that with the ample labour available, proper roads could have been made over the short distances required, and supplies brought up more rapidly.

It has been suggested that the Japanese were not averse to receiving an attack during July, being confident that their two masses could afford one another mutual support, and that neither could be overwhelmed before such support could be rendered. Again, it has been suggested that the Japanese wished to allow the Russians to concentrate before attacking them, as otherwise their enemy would only retire. It would then be necessary to follow him up, thus increasing the length of the line of communication. It has also been suggested that Oyama was awaiting the fall of Port Arthur, and the arrival of the siege corps in the field army.

The last two propositions may be disposed of at once. If Port Arthur fell, Kuropatkin would have no object in remaining so far south as Liao-yang, and might be expected to retire on Mukden, drawing the Japanese on. Secondly, two divisions remained unemployed in Japan, and large numbers of reserve formations; it can hardly be supposed, therefore, that the Japanese were awaiting the arrival of the siege corps, when they had all these troops available.

That Oyama would have witnessed a Russian offensive movement in July with complacency is probable; but, taking everything into consideration, it seems certain that supply difficulties caused the long halt.

It is not to be denied that this cause does not appear a sufficient one to many critics, particularly of the German school. Major Immanuel sums the matter up in the words, " Kurz Mangel an Wagemuth." This reason will hardly satisfy the case. Daring the Japanese leaders certainly did not lack, yet they never pursued tactically or strategically. It seems possible that, though supply difficulties were the chief obstacle, something may also be attributed to the Oriental character, which is prone to relax its energy when the immediate object is attained. The neglect to repair and keep in order the roads on the lines of communication was noticed by a very large number of observers, notably Sir Ian Hamilton, who remarks that on one occasion the ample military labour available was employed, instead of in making roads, in making an avenue up to the temporary quarters of General Kuroki. The lull in the action on the Yalu when the first effort was successful, the halt on the position of Nanshan after a loss of only some ten per cent., and other instances, tend to confirm this supposition. The moral factor had, as is always the case, a considerable share in the actions of these disciples of German methods of war.

At the end of July, Oyama suddenly pushed his left forward and seized the important railway junction of Tashichiao. Thereupon Nodzu occupied Hsimucheng, and Kuroki pushed forward over the Lan river to within two marches of Liaoyang— a position from whence he continued to threaten the left and the lines of communication of the Russians at the same time. At this time the advent of the rains obliged a further halt of nearly a month.

Situation in August The situation, however, no longer possessed the elements of danger that existed in July.

The essence of the advantage of the interior lines,

is that the divided forces of the enemy can be attacked before they can unite; but if these separated forces arrive in such a position, that they can come to one another's aid on the battlefield itself, the whole advantage of the interior lines is gone, and the situation is a positive disadvantage.

Such was the position of the Japanese after the actions of the 31st July. The dangerous period for the force operating on the exterior lines, when the Russians could turn on one portion with the bulk of their forces, and yet return in time to save the detachment left to hold the other portion from being overwhelmed, was past.

The relative timing of the advances, the methodical strategical progression from point to point, is most interesting.

In considering this war it must also be remembered that the Japanese leaders required to con-
Bearing of financial Considerations on the Japanese Strategy stantly keep in mind, the effect that the results of their operations would have on the "hard-headed" business men of London and New York, to whom the Japanese looked for the sinews of war. It is often said that want of money never yet prevented a war from being carried on. This is only a half truth. Want of money has before now often, not only prevented an outbreak of war, but induced belligerents to seek peace. To-day

the question of finance, particularly in the case of a poor country like Japan, must ever be to the front. There is little doubt that, had Japan suffered any reverse, however temporary, the rate at which she could borrow would have risen enormously, probably entirely out of proportion to the magnitude of the reverse itself.

It has excited some comment that Yinkou was not utilised as a base, at any rate after the capture of Tashichiao, and a further army, based on the Liao river, utilised to turn the Russian right. The reason for not utilising it was no doubt that the supply difficulties were already excessive with the troops actually employed.

Turning now to the Russian strategy, we have seen that their first care was to mobilise, reorganise, **The Russian** and concentrate their forces. A strong **Strategy** garrison was placed in Port Arthur and another at Vladivostok, and troops to constitute the field army were collected at Liaoyang and Haicheng.

The first point to consider is the reason for the selection of Liaoyang as the point of concentration. The town itself **Causes for** is not of great importance, but it **the Selection** **of Liaoyang** is the point of junction of the Pekin- **as a Point of** **strategical** Korea road with the railway. The ori- **Concentra-** ginal intention had been to concentrate **tion** at Harbin. The longer the Japanese line of communication the greater would be their difficulty in concentrating large bodies of troops, while the right flank of a position south of Liaoyang was dangerously near Yinkou. A concentration at Mukden or Harbin might appear more suitable therefore, and would be quite secure against an attempt of the Japanese to repeat the Prussian manœuvre of Königgrätz. The cause for the decision to push the concentration so far south is, however, not far to seek. It was vitally necessary to Russian prestige, and the eventual hope of regaining command of the sea, that Port Arthur should be relieved. " Its situation had a far-reaching effect on the general strategy of the campaign. To besiege it was a certain means of preventing the indefinite retirement of the Russian army. It was a probable means (as it actually proved) of drawing Kuropatkin into premature action. Thus it offers an illustration of a strategical lever by which the enemy's generals or his government may be moved to unwise action."[1]

The Russians, therefore, concentrated as far south as possible, pushing detachments along the railway and towards the coast, and also a strong detachment towards Korea. The operation of concentration demanded much time, and meanwhile the advance

[1] Kiggell, p. 379.

Causes for sending forward advanced Detachments of the Japanese must be opposed. This entailed a dispersion of forces. "Such a division is contrary to sound principle; but what is a general placed in such a predicament to do?"[1] The unreadiness of the Russians for war pressed like a weight on their strategy, impelling it into certain courses.

Thus we see two influences at work on the Russian strategy: first, the necessity to relieve Port Arthur; second, the necessity to gain time. In order to gain this requisite time, detachments were pushed out towards the Yalu and the coast watched from Yinkou to the mouth of the Yalu. This detachment was undoubtedly strategically correctly employed. It was intended to delay the enemy's advance, and certainly contributed to that object. As Clausewitz puts it, "The advantage of the defence is that every moment of time lost by the attacker is so much gained by the defence."

Unfortunately General Kuropatkin did not hold fast to his plan. "He allowed himself, in the course of a premeditated retreat, to be led into a series of bloody engagements,"[2] with the result that his troops began to suffer severely in moral; for though often not defeated, they always retreated, and as a consequence began not only to distrust their generals,[3] but to distrust themselves.

[1] Kiggell, p. 368.   [2] R. M. G. (1906), vol. i. 106.
[3] R. d' A., vol. lxvii. 382

Of these adventures undoubtedly the most serious blunder was the despatch of Stakelberg with 30,000 men to attack Oku with 40,000. Not only was this move contrary to the general plan, but also it was a half measure. It would have been possible to place at Stakelberg's disposal about 50,000 men for this advance, and it is not too much to say that in such a movement would have lain the germ of a temporary success; at that period even a temporary success would have been of great value.

After that adventure, with the exception of certain reconnaissances in force, Kuropatkin's strategy was purely defensive. Towards the end of July he had available a force equivalent to five army corps and three cavalry divisions. A sixth army corps was rapidly arriving. What was to be done with this mass? Colonel Kiggell answers this question with the words, "Victory can only be won by striking."

The Russians having collected an Army, what should be done with it?

This was evidently realised by Kuropatkin, who had the following courses open to him: first, to oppose Kuroki with a force about equal to an army corps, hold Nodzu near Hsimucheng in check, and take the offensive with the remainder of his troops (about 75,000) against Oku, who had at that time four divisions and a cavalry brigade, in all some 60,000 men. In view of General Nodzu's proximity with 20,000 this course was dangerous. Secondly, he could reverse the operations, holding the southern force and attacking Kuroki. Thirdly, he could press forward into the gap between the two Japanese bodies, and thus threaten the communications of both. This latter operation required a high degree of manœuvring capacity, which the Russians did not possess. There was a last alternative. The right flank of the whole Japanese army was formed of the 12th Division and a portion of the Guards reserve brigade. Its situation at Chiaotou, on the direct road via Penhsihu and Bianyupusa to Mukden, was a standing menace to the Russian line of communication. This body was isolated to some extent, and its right flank was not far from Penhsihu, where stood a brigade of Cossacks. It was possible to attack it. This was the offensive action Kuropatkin decided to limit himself to. For the task the X. Corps was detailed, and proceeded to carry out the movement—by occupying a "position."

To what extent the cult of positions, for it almost amounted to a cult, was carried by the **Russian Position Tactics** Russians may be judged when one considers that this corps which was taking the offensive (save the mark!) against an isolated Japanese division provided itself with "advanced," "main," "intermediate," and "rear" "positions." Truly might Freiherr von Tettau exclaim, that the battle of Yushuling is a first-rate example of the crippling effect of the "war of positions" on the will to adopt a determined course of action.[1]

It has been said that the antidote to entrenchments is manœuvre, and it was certainly demonstrated in this war by the Japanese. The positions at Kaiping, at Haicheng, on the Fenshuiling and the Motienling, fell to the simple threat of a flank attack.

Throughout the war the same thing recurs. We meet it in Bilderling's advance on the Sha river; and in August, when Kuropatkin had ordered an advance (which the Japanese forestalled), Freiherr von Tettau remarks that General Sluchevski said to him, "How lucky that Vassilieff had not already put his corps in motion forward, for otherwise he would have come upon the Japanese when on the march, where we had no 'position.'"

This seems to have been the general view of the offensive taken by most of the Russian generals.

Thus the favourable moment was allowed to pass, and Kuropatkin decided to await his opponents' onslaught against his carefully-prepared entrenched camp at Liaoyang. The Russian strategy was affected early in the war by a contempt for their

[1] F. v. T., i. 231.

opponents, later by a fear of them. Neither affection improved their strategy.[1]

This chapter would not be complete without a reference to the intelligence departments of either side.

Information and Secrecy
Even to this time to a very large extent we are ignorant of the numbers and lines of communications of the Japanese in Manchuria in 1904-1905. It was very different with the Russians. In a paper translated and issued by our general staff, entitled "The Importance of Secrecy in War," written by Lieut.-Colonel Izmestiev of the Russian General Staff, we see something of the guilelessness of the Russian methods. Every detail connected with the mobilisation, numbers, command, and situation of the troops was published not only in the non-official press, but also in the *Russki Invalid*, and he sums up: "In short, the censor's department of the headquarter staff had no clear idea as to what kind of information might be given to the public and what might not." Undoubtedly, too, the Japanese utilised their affinity to the Chinese to aid them in their secret service.

So much so is this the case that, in criticising the measures taken by the respective armies, it should be constantly remembered that the Russians

[1] F. v. T., p. 270.

were surrounded by the usual fog of war, but the Japanese information was so good that for them the fog was little more than a light mist.

The German principle, that the initiative of the subordinate leaders is not to be interfered with was **Initiative of Subordinates** kept constantly before the eyes of the Japanese. Kuropatkin acted quite differently, interfering in every detail, however minute—a proceeding which, naturally, paralysed the action of subordinate generals.[1]

The strategical lessons of the war have now been briefly reviewed, and during the narrative some **General tactical Remarks** slight comments were made on the tactics of the various engagements. It may, however, be repeated that the offensive, even in frontal attacks on prepared positions, was constantly finally successful, and that approaches to these positions were constantly, and attacks on them occasionally, made at night. The enfilade fire of a few guns or rifles succeeded in making a whole position untenable. When passive defence is a necessity, communications and roads must be most carefully attended to, a *position de repli* previously prepared, and units detailed for its occupation.

The importance of concealment was again demonstrated. The lessons of the South African War

[1] For a good example, which occurred in August, see F. v. T., i. 301.

were, in fact, repeated; though it must be admitted that, up to the end of July 1904, the Japanese still attacked in dense lines, and with supports in closed columns.[1]

In the conduct of their battles both Oku and Kuroki seem to have always aimed at attacking the front and both flanks at the same time. The Japanese do not seem, with occasional exceptions, to have endeavoured to utilise their apparently considerable superiority in manœuvre. This consideration has been touched upon before in the comments on the various engagements.

The fact that the Japanese did not follow up their victories by a tactical pursuit has been much commented on. The fact is that the Russians were hardly ever so severely defeated as to permit of pursuit. Pursuit must be undertaken by cavalry or fresh infantry. In the former the Japanese were numerically weak; the latter were not forthcoming at the end of the battles, for in almost every case the Japanese generals had put in their last man before the victory was gained.

Pursuits

The lack of success of the Russian cavalry was obvious, and seems to have been due largely to the following causes:—

Cavalry

1. Bad instruction of the men and the unsuitability of Cossacks for reconnaissance. Frei-

[1] Conferences, Fasicule, ii. 64.

herr von Tettau draws from this the conclusion that *landwehr* (or yeomanry) cavalry will not be of much use in modern war.

2. The country was bad for cavalry. Large forces were, it is said, only able to move at a walk,[1] and even small bodies could only get along slowly. The streams were liable to sudden floods, and the forage was poor. Long-distance patrols, if they returned at all, brought in their news too late.

3. Bad maps.

Raids The only raid on the communications attempted by the Cossacks has been referred to in Chapter II.

Of the reasons adduced for the cavalry failure the first is probably the most important, for good service was done by the railway (or frontier) guards and by the mounted scout detachments.

The Japanese cavalry found the same difficulty in rapid movements as the Russians, yet it took a fair share in the service of security, in which, assisted by infantry, it was remarkably successful.

Artillery With regard to the employment of the guns, it may be permissible to quote Major Geddes:—

" As regards the Japanese, the campaign in Manchuria was begun upon the principle of concentrating guns, but the necessity and advantages of

[1] J. S. M., 10th series, vol. xxvi. 321.

dispersion were soon recognised. That dispersion was a necessity was proved in the hilly country, where even if a position for six batteries in line were forthcoming, the probability was that from one flank, or perhaps from both flanks, the target was invisible or the range too great."[1]

"At the commencement of the campaign the artillery came into action at very long ranges (5000 to 6000 yards), and seldom moved forward to support the infantry attack. . . . The guns were entrenched, and indirect laying the rule. At the battles of Telissu and Tashichiao the Japanese artillery, endeavouring to press forward in support of the infantry, lost so many horses that they had to desist. . . . Thus it may be concluded that artillery, once committed to a certain position, may have to remain there until nightfall."[2]

The Japanese were careful of their guns. Sir Ian Hamilton remarks: "The Japanese are lavish with their brave infantry, and think little of losing two or three hundred men, but wrap up their artillery in cotton wool to the extent of not giving the infantry the full support they are entitled to expect."

The value to the defence of having a few guns to push up to the crest in support of the infantry during the close attack has been touched on. It seems also valuable to push forward a few guns

[1] Geddes, 31. [2] Geddes, 43.

with the attack where the ground permits. Pack artillery seems peculiarly suited for this purpose.[1]

The high explosive shell of the Japanese had singularly small effect.[2]

L'Envoi

In the preface to an article in the *Revue Militaire Générale*, General Langlois points out that certain immutable principles of war were again established in Manchuria in 1904. They are:

1. The preponderating influence of the moral factor.

2. The superiority of the offensive over the defensive.

3. That unity of effort is an essential to success. Half measures only lead to failure.

To attain these objects the commander must make his subordinates understand his wishes and leave them to carry them out. To make his presence felt the commander must keep in hand and use his reserve.

For the subordinate generals, and indeed for every subordinate, it is necessary to never lose sight of the main object of the commander. In unity is strength.

These words seem a fitting termination to this volume.

[1] See R. U. S. I. Journal, vol. li. 721. Article by Major Knapp, R.H.A. Also vol. lii. 32. Lecture by Captain Vincent, R.H.A.
[2] F. v. T., i. 218.

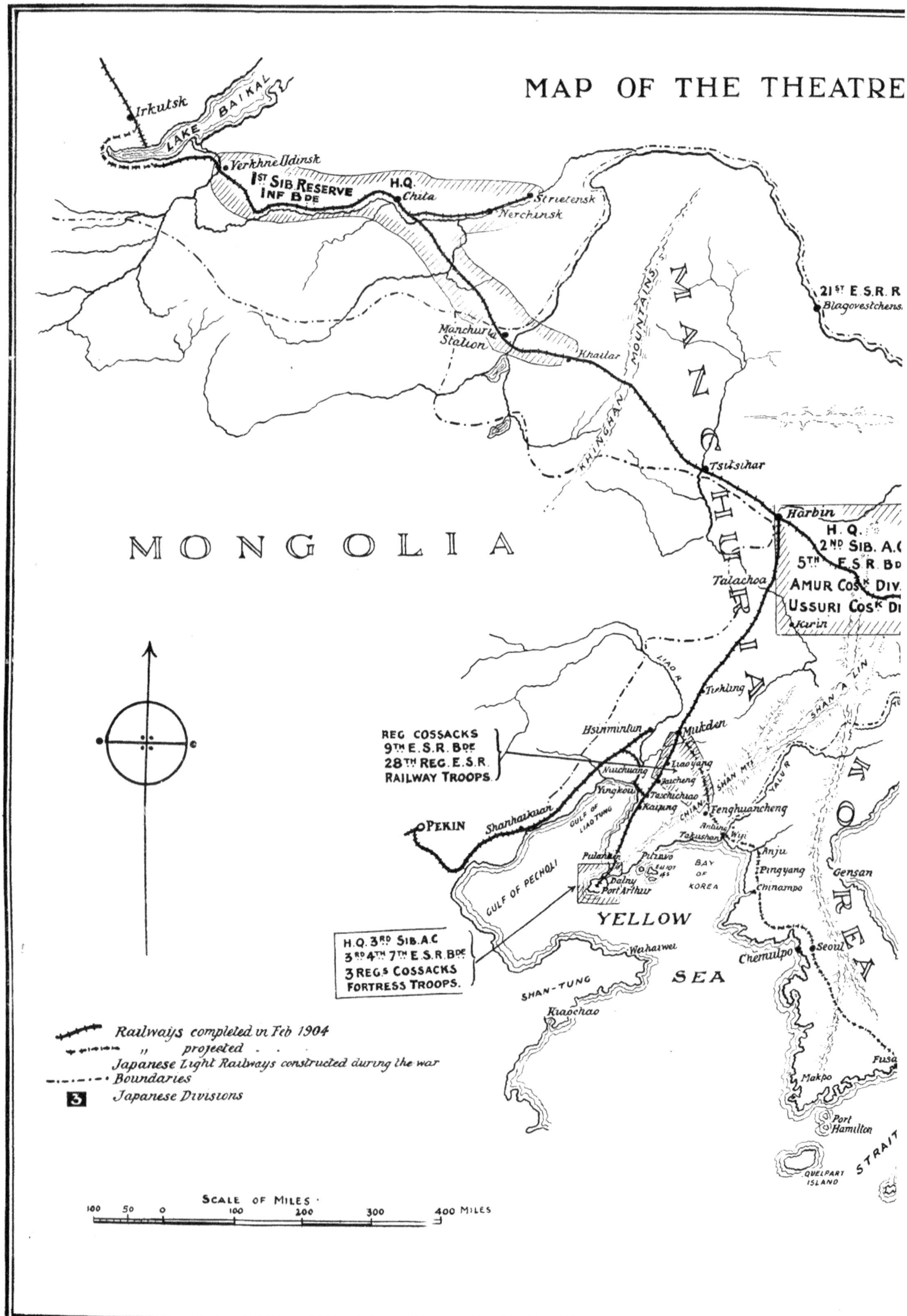

SWAN SONNENSCHEIN & CO. LTD. LONDON.

MAP I.

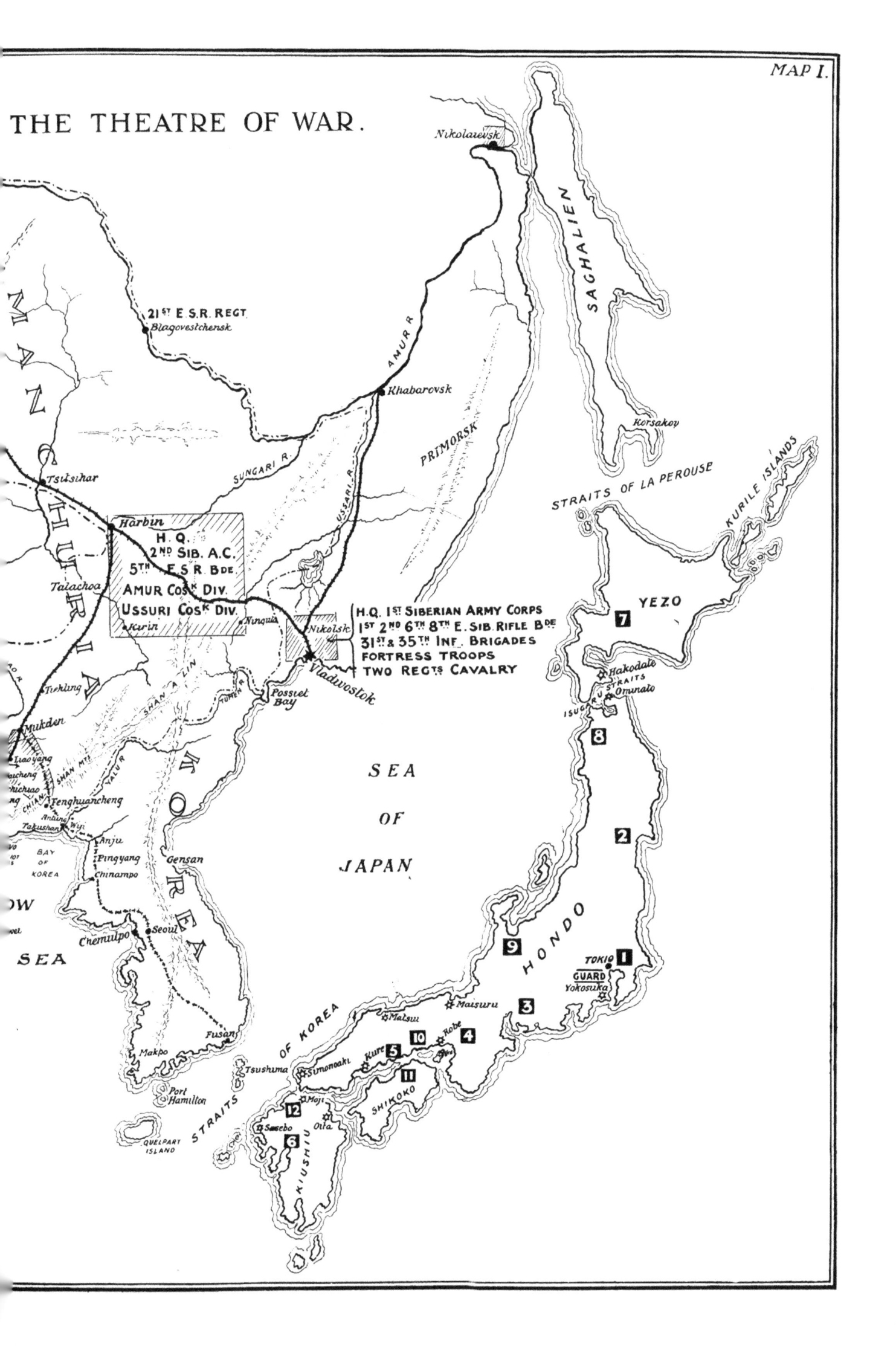

THE THEATRE OF WAR.

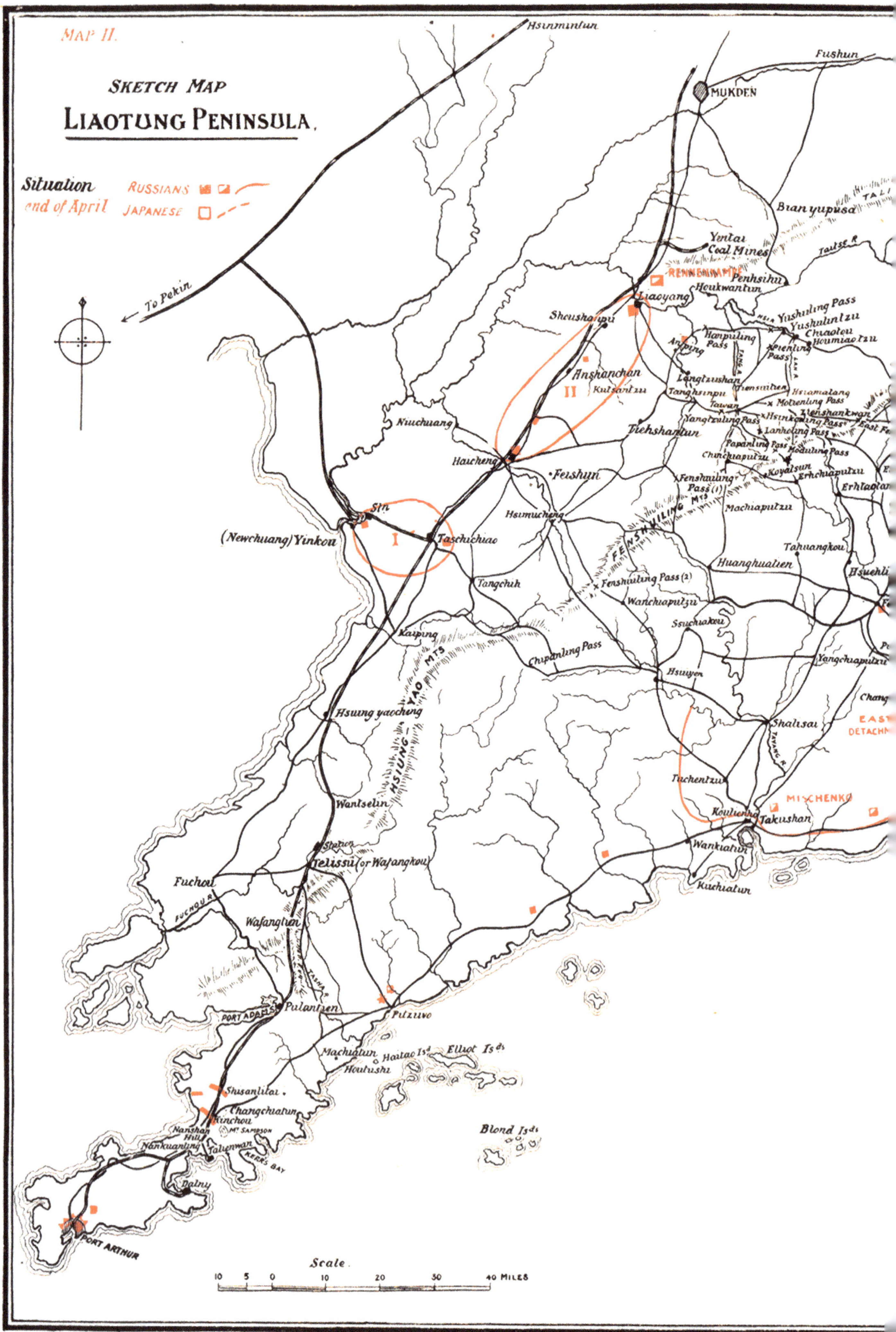

SWAN SONNENSCHEIN & Co. Ltd. LONDON.

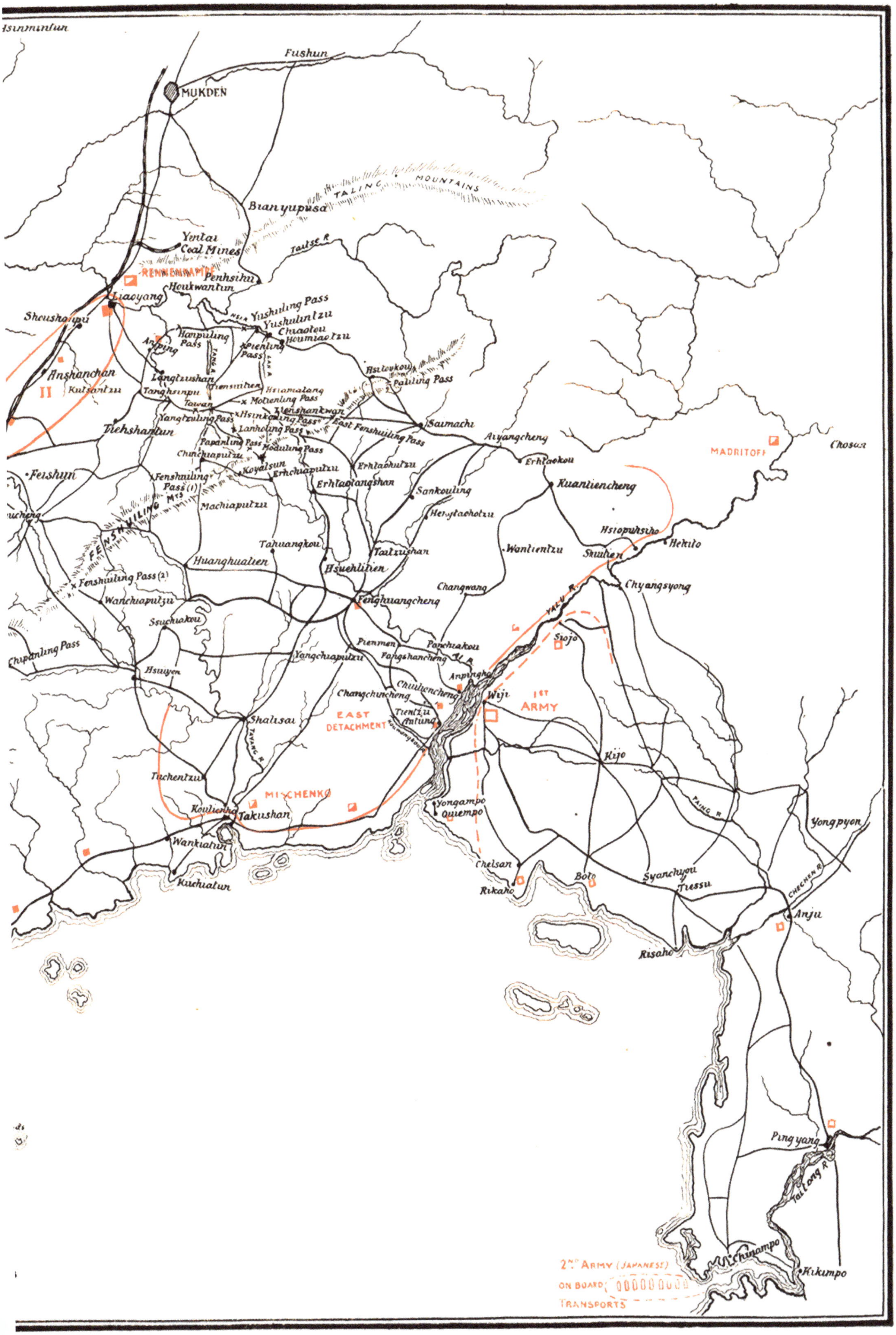
Fushun
MUKDEN
TALING MOUNTAINS
Bian yupusa
Yentai Coal Mines
Taitse R.
RENNENKAMPFF
Penhsihu
Houkwantun
Liaoyang
Sheushanpu
Yushuling Pass
Yushulintzu
Chiaotou
Houmiaotzu
Hanpuling Pass
Anping
Pienling Pass
Anshanchan
II
Kutsantzu
Langtzushan
Hsiaoukou
Paliling Pass
Tienshuitien
Hsiamatang
Tanghsinpu
Tawan
Motienling Pass
Tienshankwan
Yangtzuling Pass
Hsinkailing Pass
East Fenshuiling Pass
Saimachi
Lanholing Pass
Tiehshantun
Papanling Pass
Modulung Pass
Aiyangcheng
Chinchiaputzu
Koyatsun
Erhchiaputzu
Erhtaohutzu
Erhtaokou
Chosan
MADRITOFF
Feishuin
Fenshuiling Pass (1)
Erhtaotangshan
Kuantiencheng
Sankouling
Machiaputzu
FENSHUILING MTS
Hengtaohotzu
Hsiopuhsiho
Tahuangkou
Taitzushan
Wantientzu
Hekito
Shutien
Huanghualien
Hsuehlitien
Fenshuiling Pass (2)
Changwang
Chyangsyong
Wanchiaputzu
Fenghuangcheng
YALU R.
Ssuchiakou
Siojo
Pienmen
Panchiakou
Chipanling Pass
Yangchiaputzu
Fangshancheng
Anpingho
Hsuiyen
Chiuliencheng
Changchuncheng
Wiju
1ST ARMY
EAST DETACHMENT
Tientzu
Antung
Shalisai
Kijo
Tachentzu
MI^SCHENKO
Koulienho
Takushan
Yongampo
Quiempo
Yongpyon
Wankiatun
Chelsan
Rikako
Boto
Syanchyou
Tiessu
Kuchiatun
Anju
Risaho
CHECHEN R.
Ping yang
Tai tong R
2ND ARMY (JAPANESE)
ON BOARD TRANSPORTS
Chinampo
Kikumpo

MAP III

BATTLE OF THE YALU SITUATION DAWN 1ST MAY 1904.

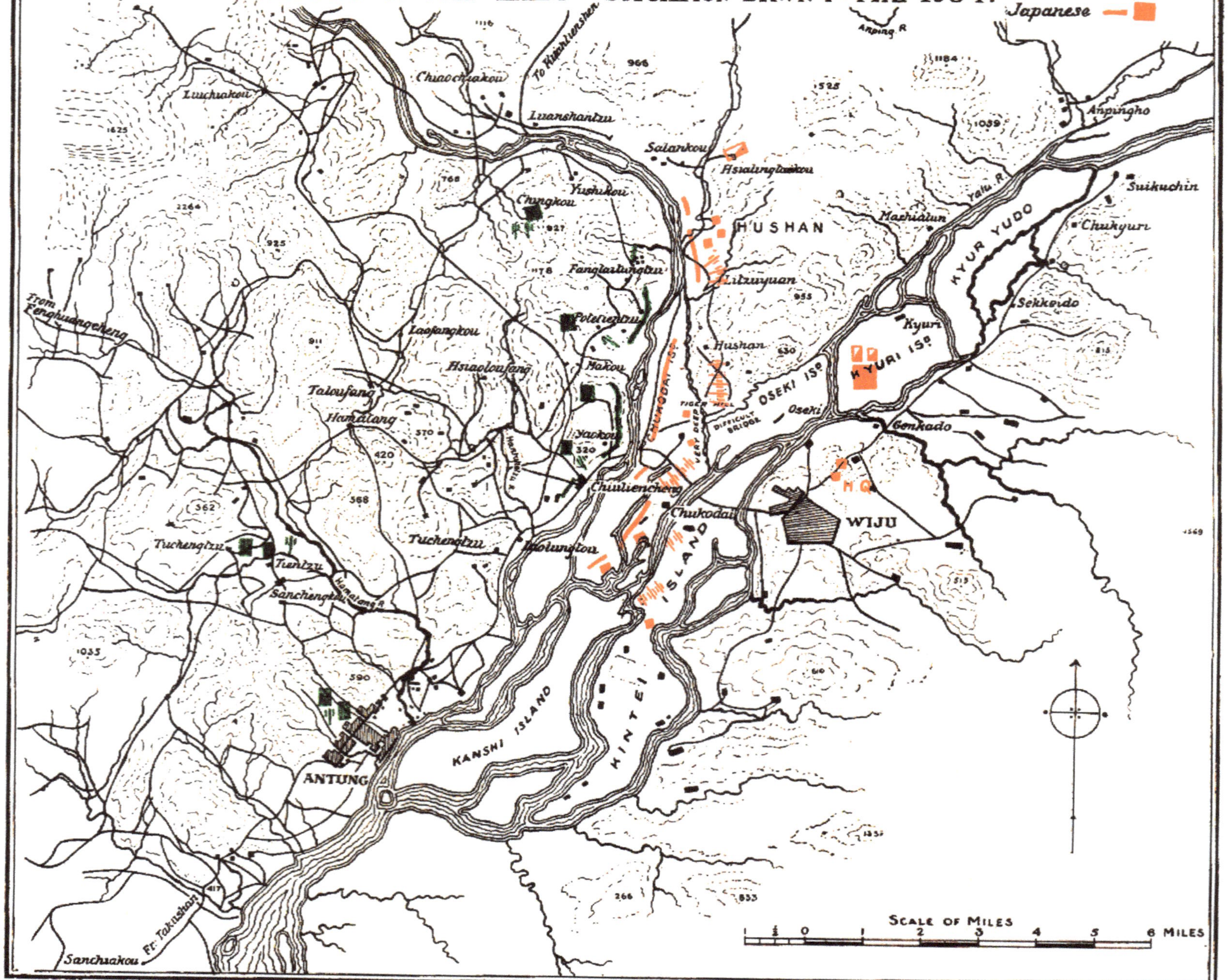

SWAN SONNENSCHEIN & CO. LTD LONDON.

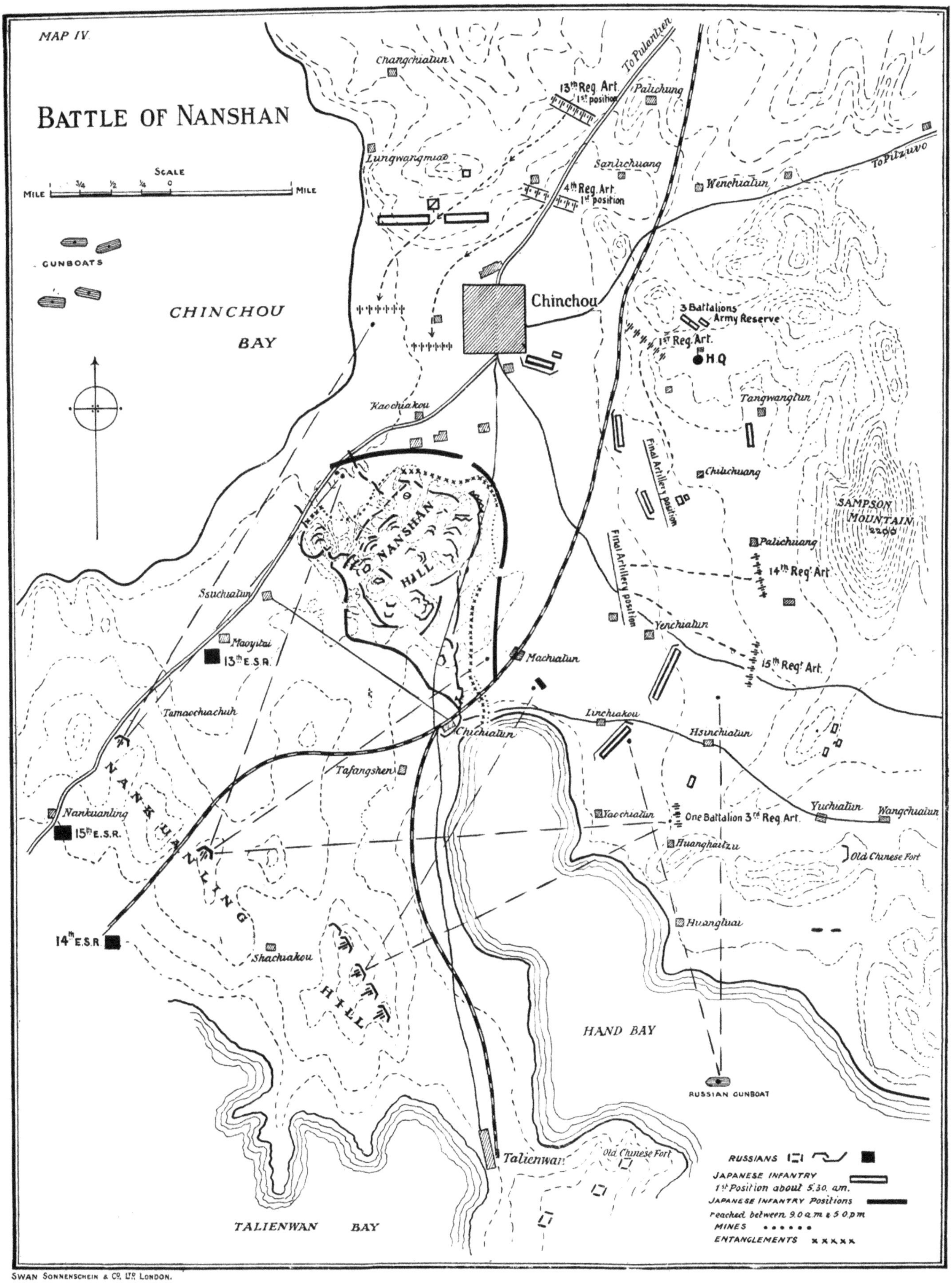

SWAN SONNENSCHEIN & Co. LTD. LONDON.

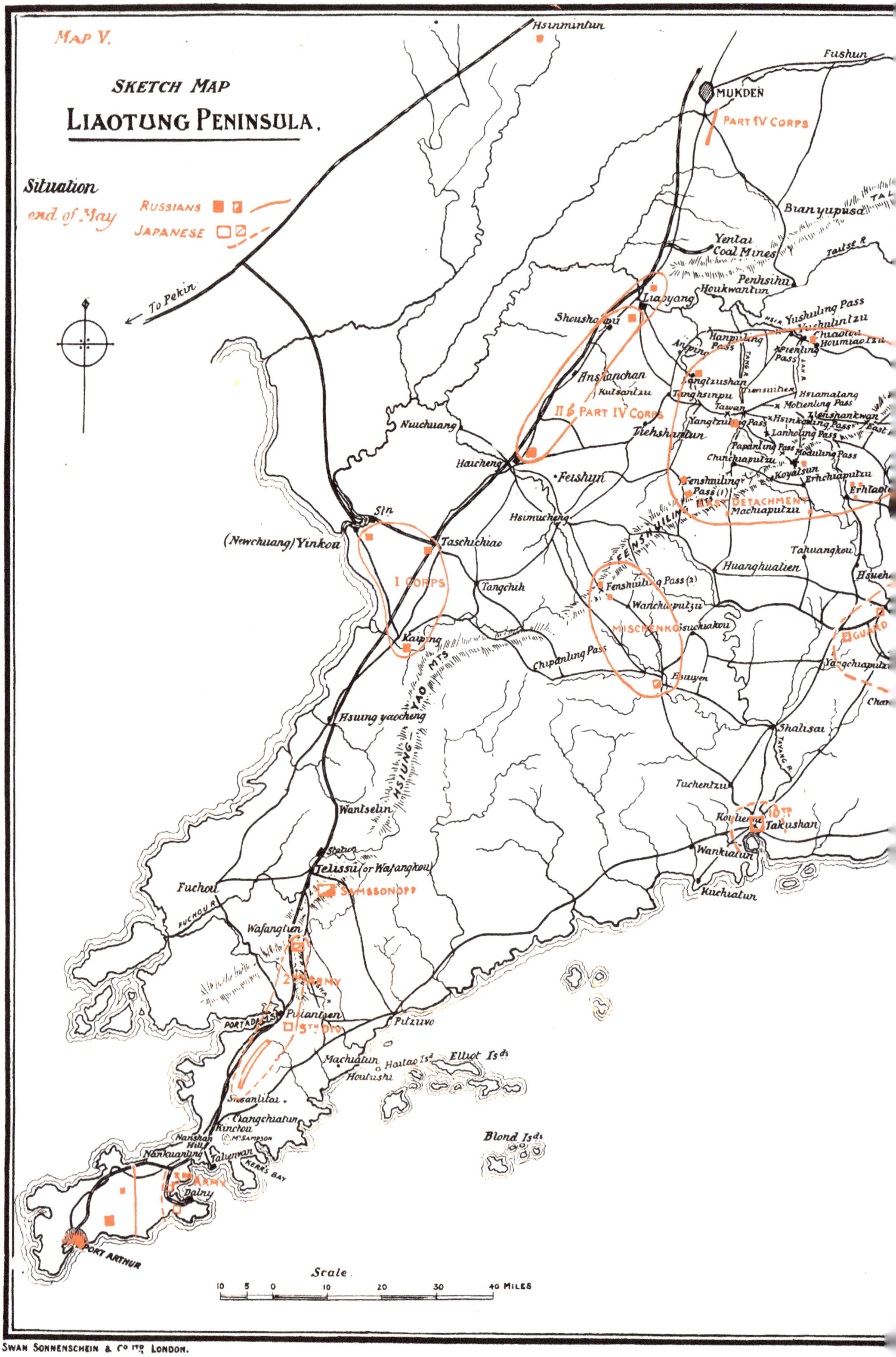

SWAN SONNENSCHEIN & Co LTD LONDON.

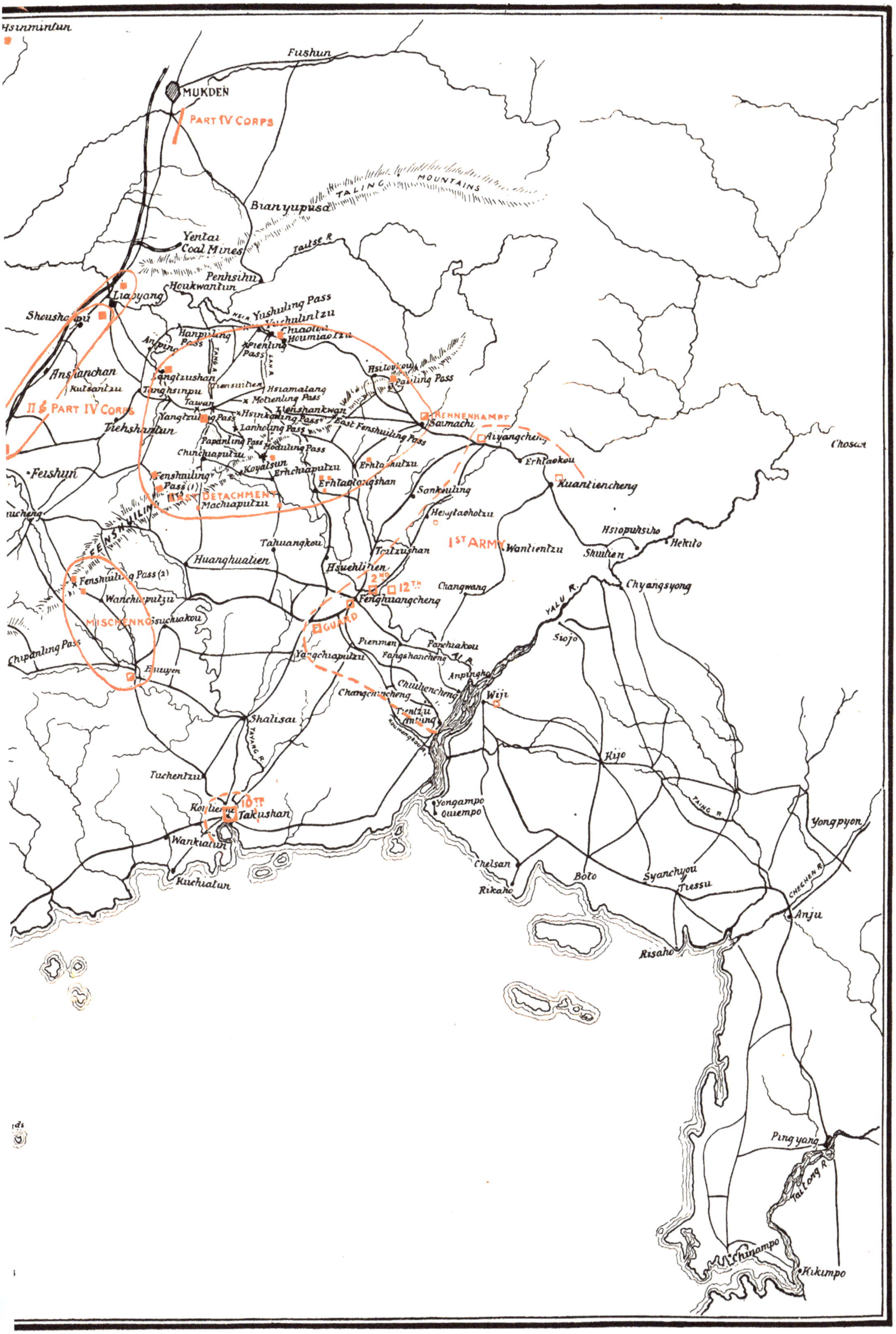

Hsinmintun
Fushun
MUKDEN
PART IV CORPS
TALING MOUNTAINS
Bianyupusa
Yentai Coal Mines
Taitse R.
Penhsihu
Houkwantun
Liaoyang
Shoushanpu
Yushuling Pass
Anshanchan
Kutsantzu
II & PART IV CORPS
Tiehshantun
Feishun
Tangtzushan
Tanghsinpu
Tawan
Yangtzuling Pass
Papanling Pass
Chinchiaputzu
Fenshuiling Pass (1)
1ST DETACHMENT
Machiaputzu
Motienling Pass
Lienshankwan
Lanholing Pass
Modulung Pass
Koyaisun
Erhchiaputzu
Erhtaolongshan
Hsitowkou
Pailing Pass
RENNENKAMPF
Saimachi
East Fenshuiling Pass
Aiyangcheng
Erhtaokou
Kuantiencheng
Chosen
Sankouling
Hengtaohotzu
1ST ARMY
Wantientzu
Shuitien
Hsiopuhsiho
Hekito
Chyangsyong
Tahuangkou
Huanghualien
Hsuehlitien
Teitzushan
2ND
12TH
Changwang
Fenghuangcheng
FENSHUILING
Fenshuiling Pass (2)
Wanchiaputzu
MISCHENKO
Chipanling Pass
Hsiuyen
GUARD
Yangchiaputzu
Pienmen
Fangshancheng
Panchiakou
Anpingho
Changchiencheng
Chiulienchneg
Wiju
YALU R.
Siojo
Antung
Shalisai
TAYANG R.
Tuchentzu
10TH
Takushan
Wankiatun
Kuchiatun
Yongampo
Quiempo
Kijo
TAING R.
Yongpyon
Chelsan
Rikaho
Boto
Syanchyou
Tiessu
CHECHEN R.
Anju
Risaho
Ping yang
Tai tong R.
Chinampo
Kikimpo

MAP VI.

BATTLE OF TE-LI-SSU (OR WA-FANG-KOU)

SITUATION AT DAWN ON JUNE 15TH 1904.

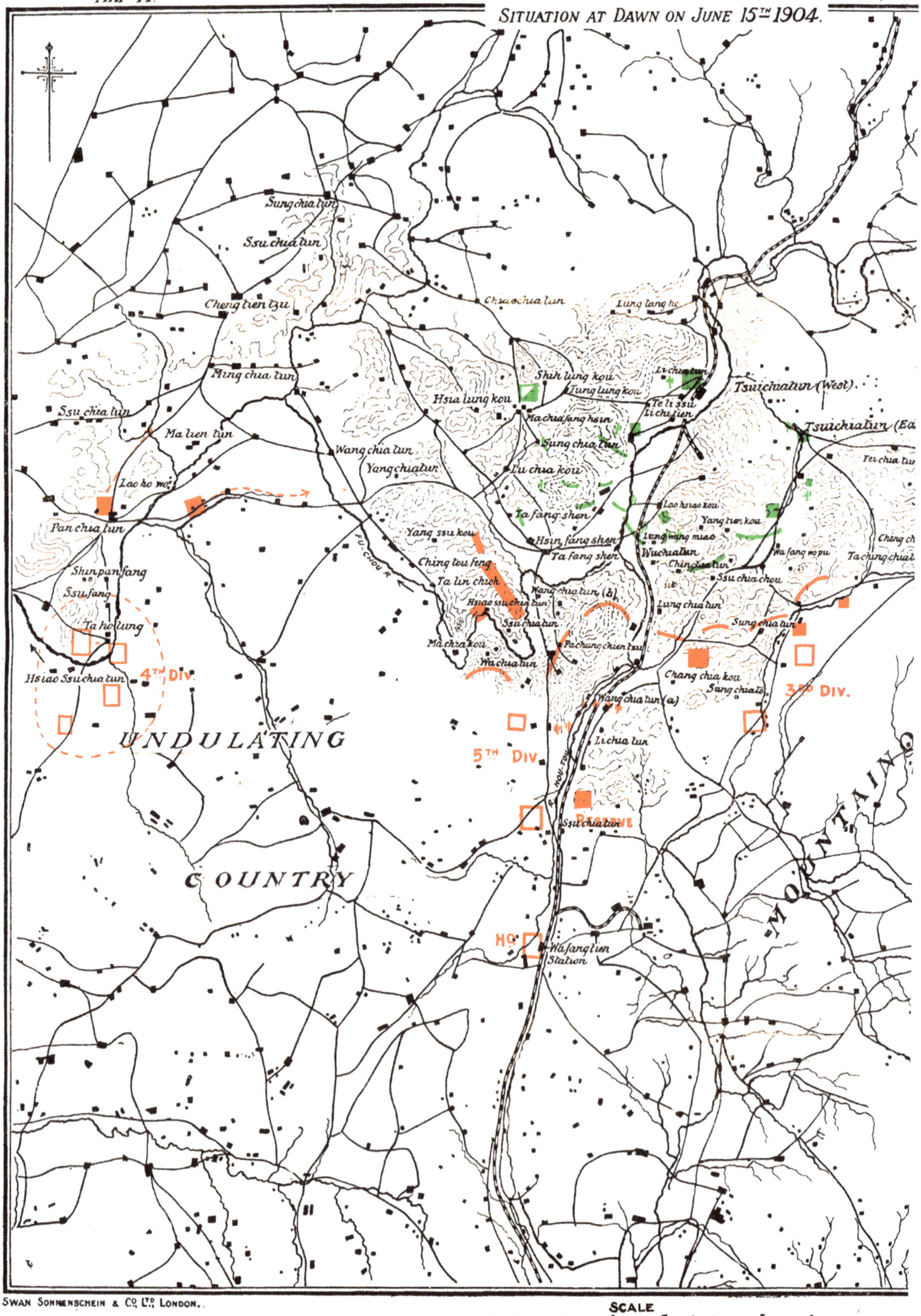

SWAN SONNENSCHEIN & CO. LTD. LONDON.

SCALE

1 ½ 0 1 2 3 4 5 6 MILES

Battle of Te-li-ssu (or Wa-fang-kou)

Situation at Dawn on June 15th 1904.

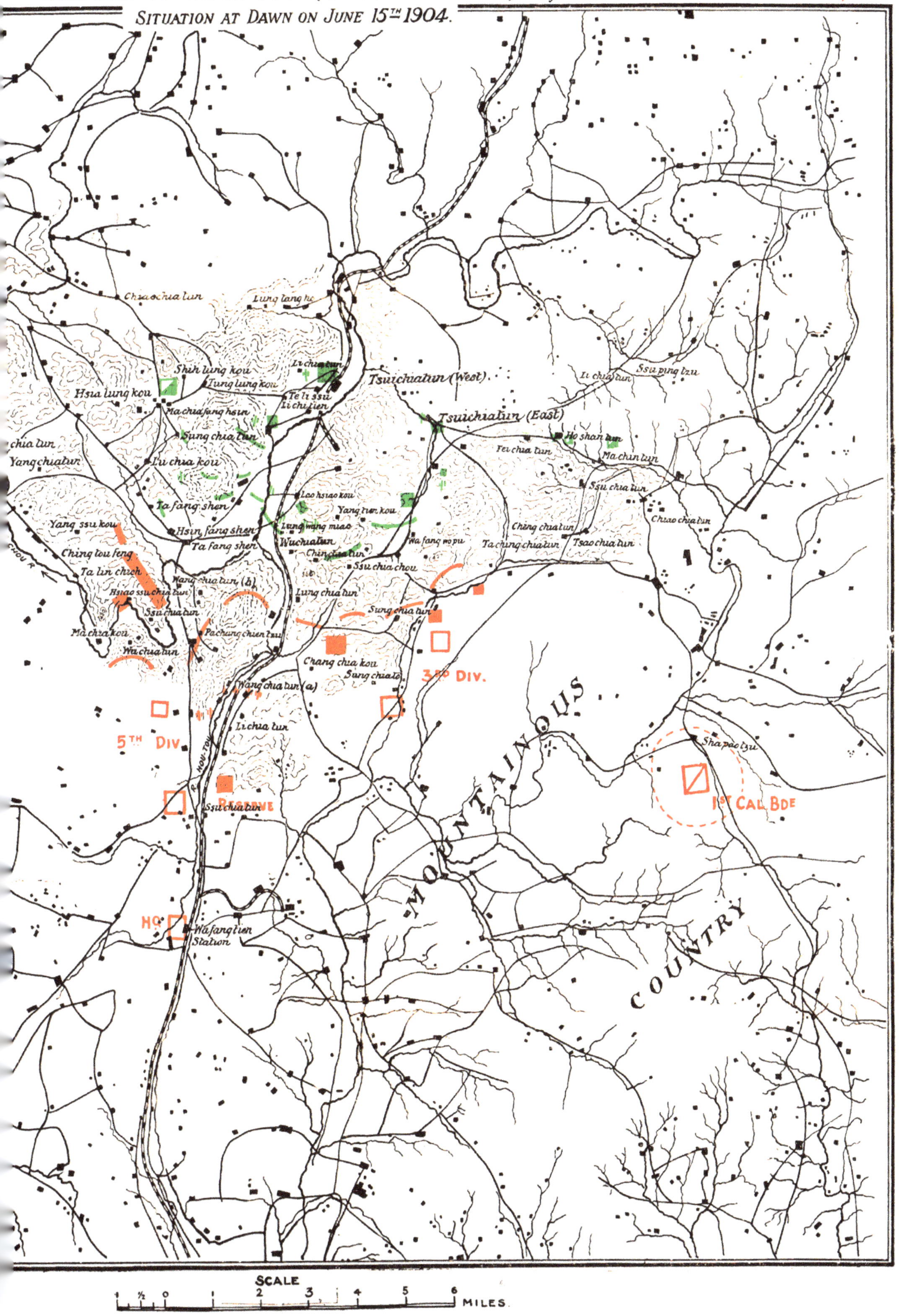

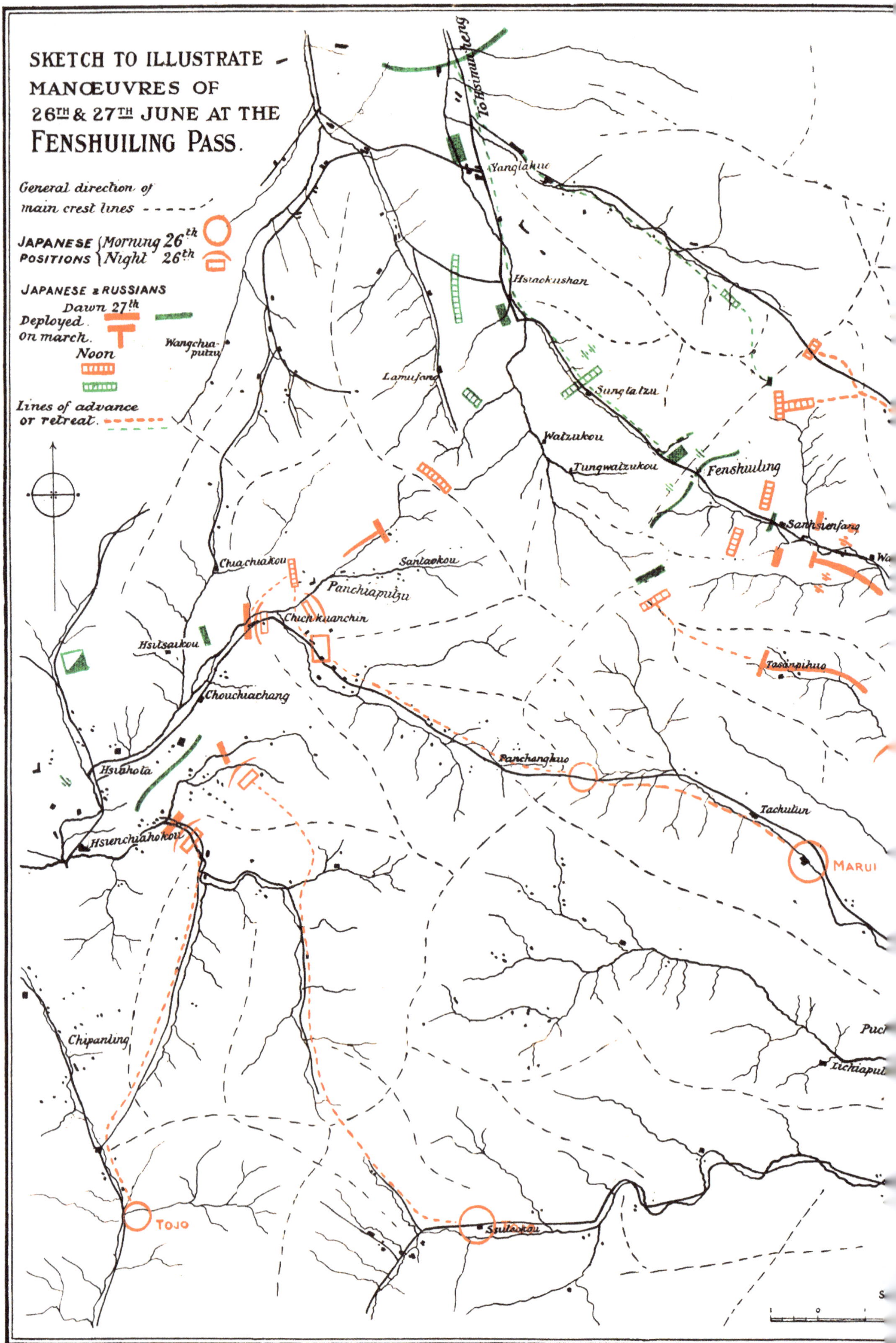

SWAN SONNENSCHEIN & Co. Ld., LONDON.

MAP VII

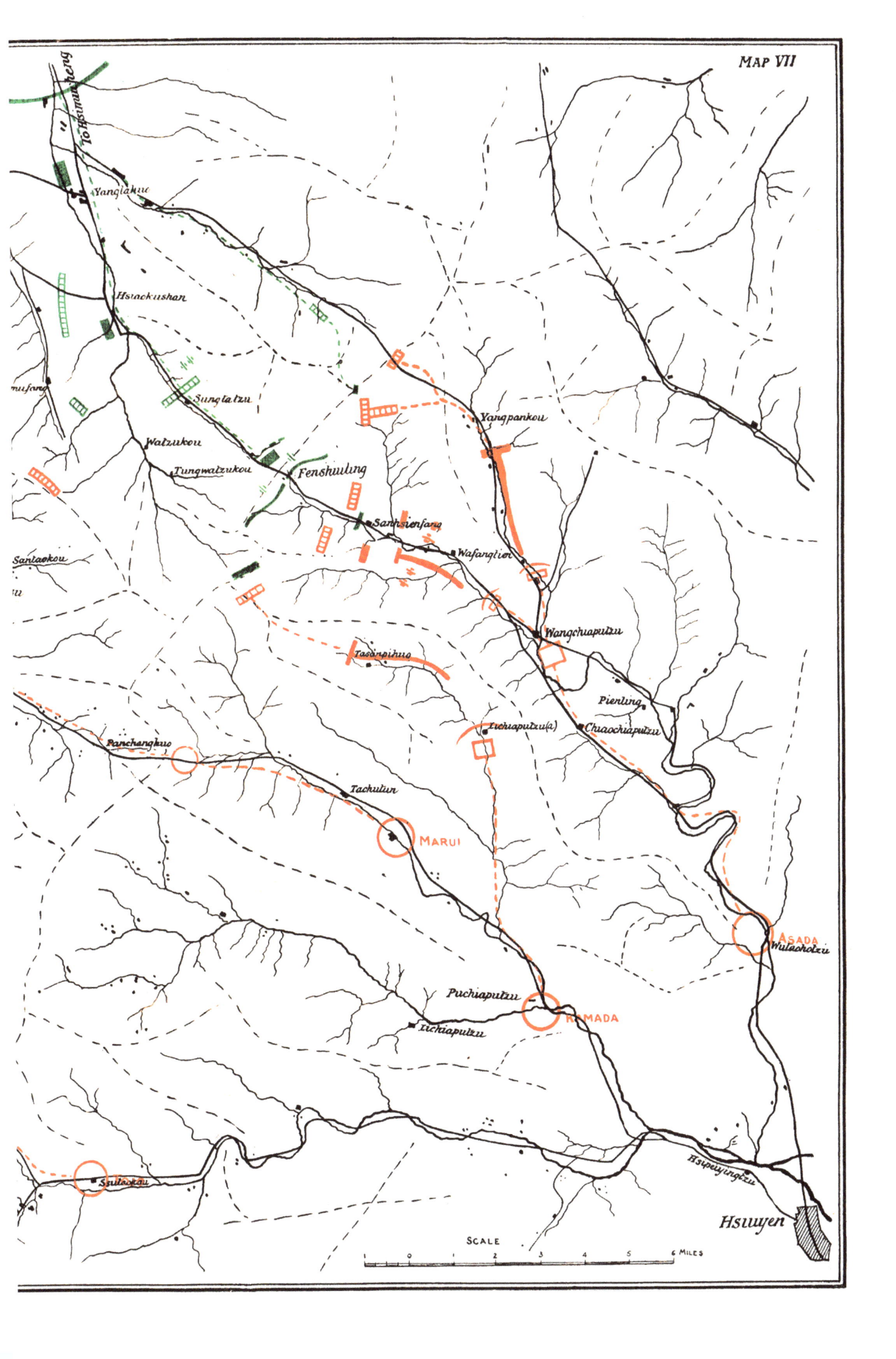

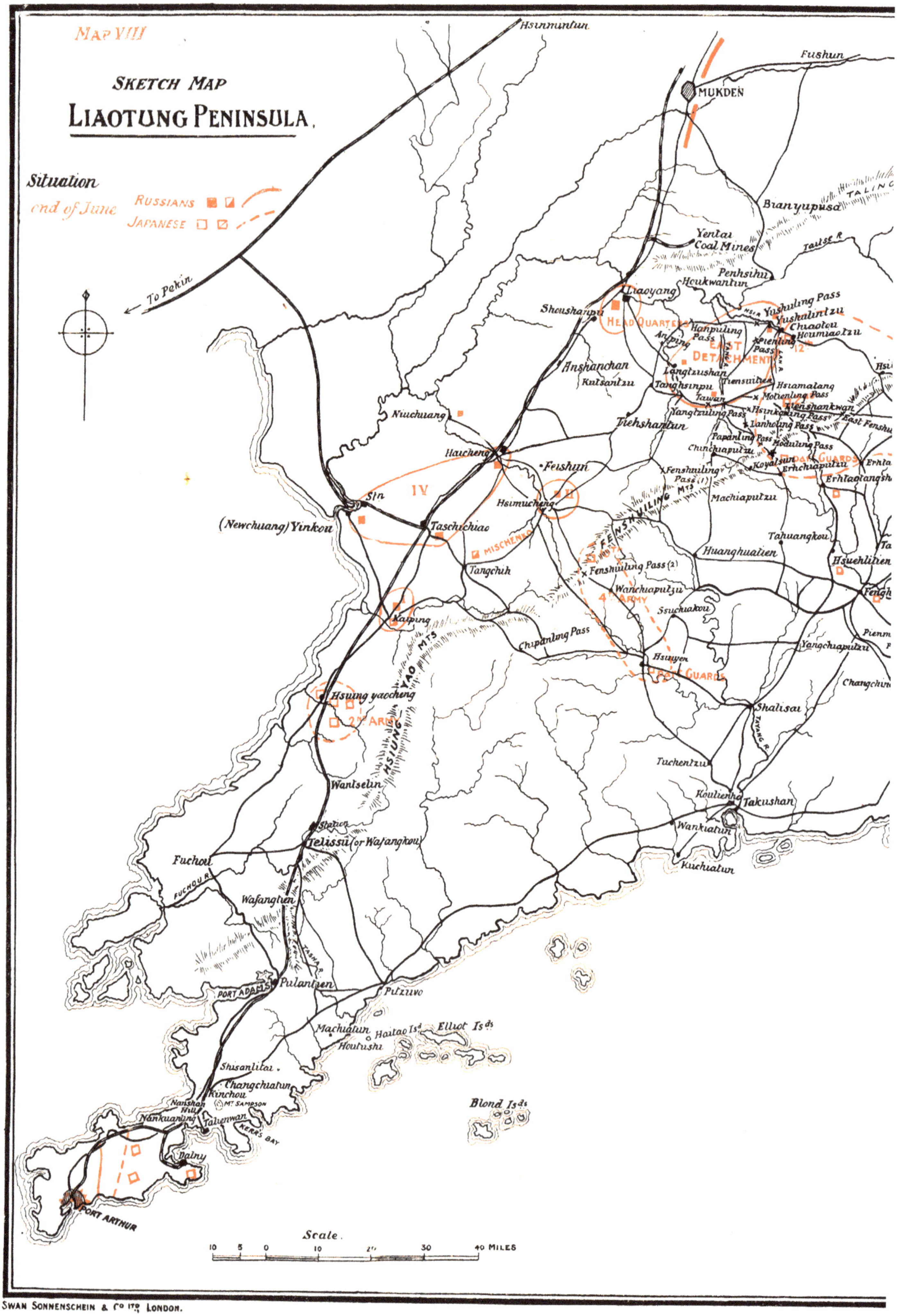

SWAN SONNENSCHEIN & Co. Ltd. LONDON.

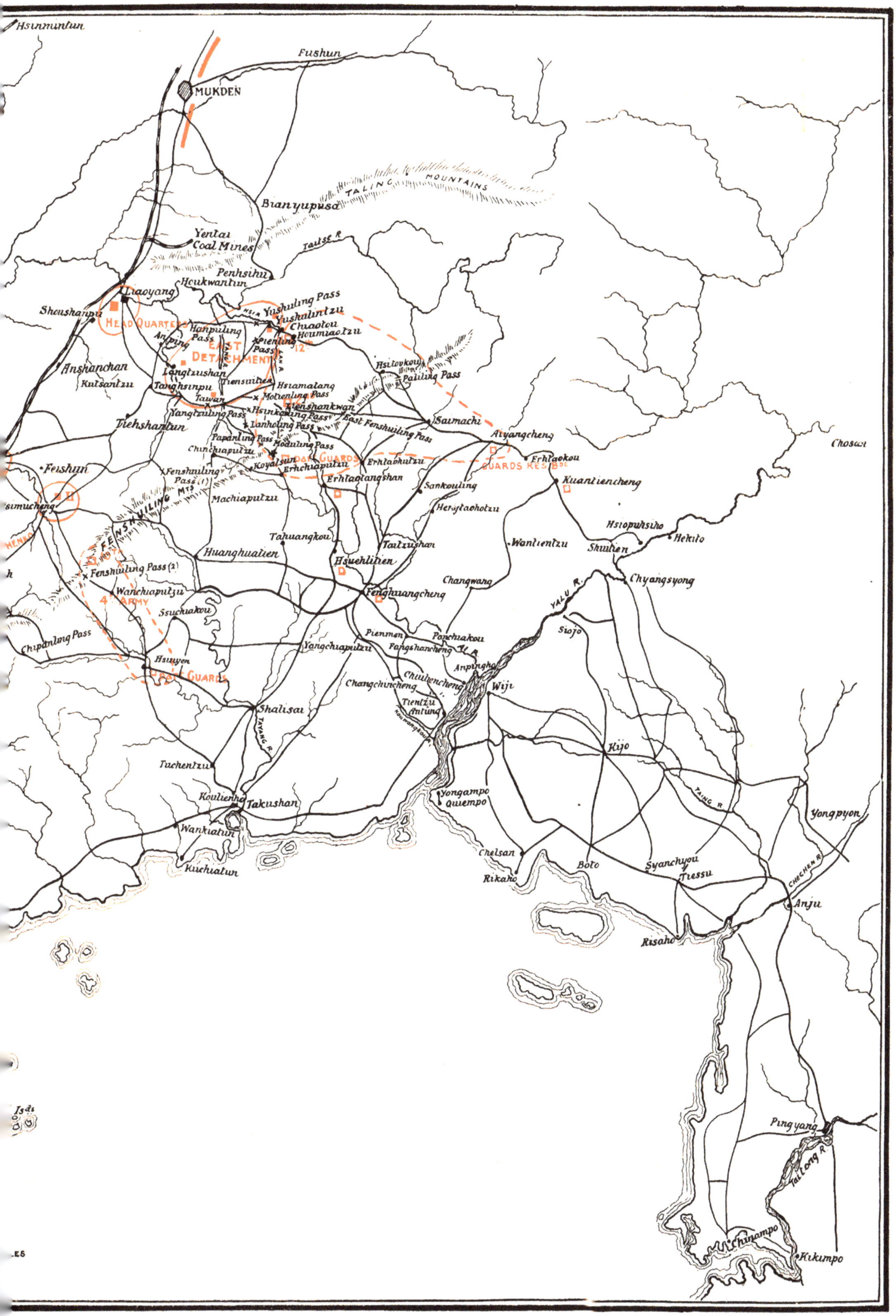

Hsinmintun
Fushun
MUKDEN
TALING MOUNTAINS
Bianyupuso
Yentai Coal Mines
Taitse R
Penhsihu
Houkwantun
Liaoyang
Shoushanpu
HEAD QUARTERS
Yushuling Pass
Yushulintzu
Chiaotou
Houmiaotzu
Hanpuling Pass
Anping
EAST DETACHMENT
Pienling Pass
12
Anshanchan
Langtzushan
Kutsantzu
Tanghsinpu
Tiensuitien
Hsiamatang
Hsitovkou
Pailing Pass
Motienling Pass
Tawan
Tienshankwan
Yangtzuling Pass
Hsinkailing Pass
East Fenshuiling Pass
Saimachi
Lanholing Pass
Tiehshantun
Papanling Pass
Koduling Pass
Aiyangcheng
Chinchiaputzu
Koyatsun
GUARDS
Erhchiaputzu
Erhtaohutzu
GUARDS RES. Bde
Erhtaokou
Chosen
Feishun
Fenshuiling Pass (1)
Erhtaotangshan
Kuantiencheng
Sankouling
Simucheng
FENSHUILING MTS
Machiaputzu
Hengtaohotzu
Hsiopuhsiho
Tahuangkou
Hekito
Taitzushan
Wantientzu
Shuitien
Huanghuatien
Hsuehlitien
Fenshuiling Pass (2)
Changwang
Chyangsyong
Wanchiaputzu
4th ARMY
YALU R.
Fenghuangcheng
Ssuchiakou
Siojo
Chipanling Pass
Pienmen
Panchiakou
Yangchiaputzu
Fangshancheng
Hsuiyen
Anpingho
GUARDS
Chiulienching
Changchincheng
Wiju
Shalisai
Tientzu
Antung
Taiyang R
Kijo
Tuchentzu
Taing R
Koulienho
Takushan
Yongampo
Quiempo
Yongpyon
Wankiatun
Chelsan
Boto
Syanchyou
Kuchiatun
Rikaho
Tessu
Chechen R
Anju
Risaho
Isds
Pingyang
Tatong R
Chinampo
Kikimpo

MAP II

BATTLE OF TASHIHCHIAO

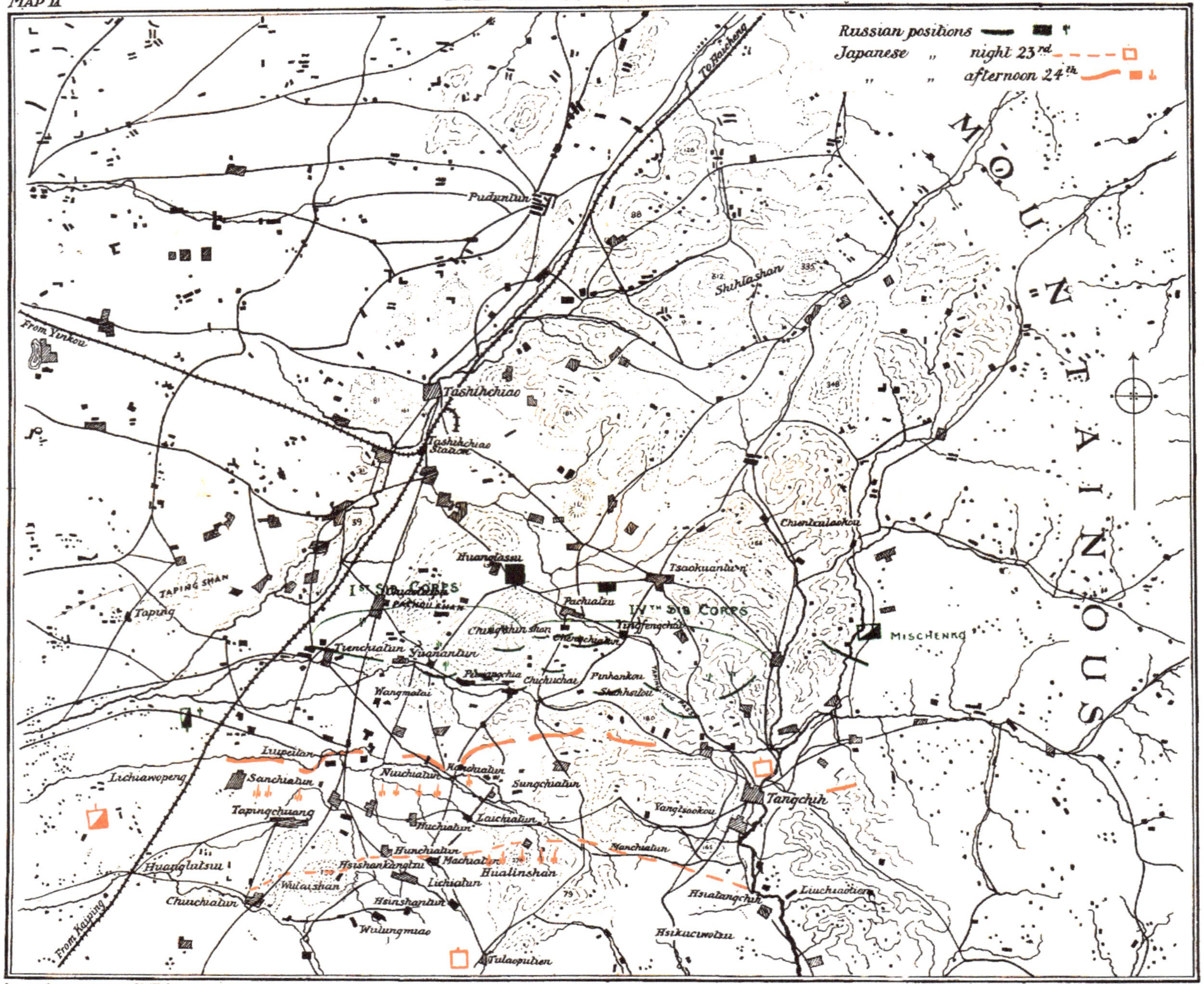

Swan Sonnenschein & Co. Ltd. London.

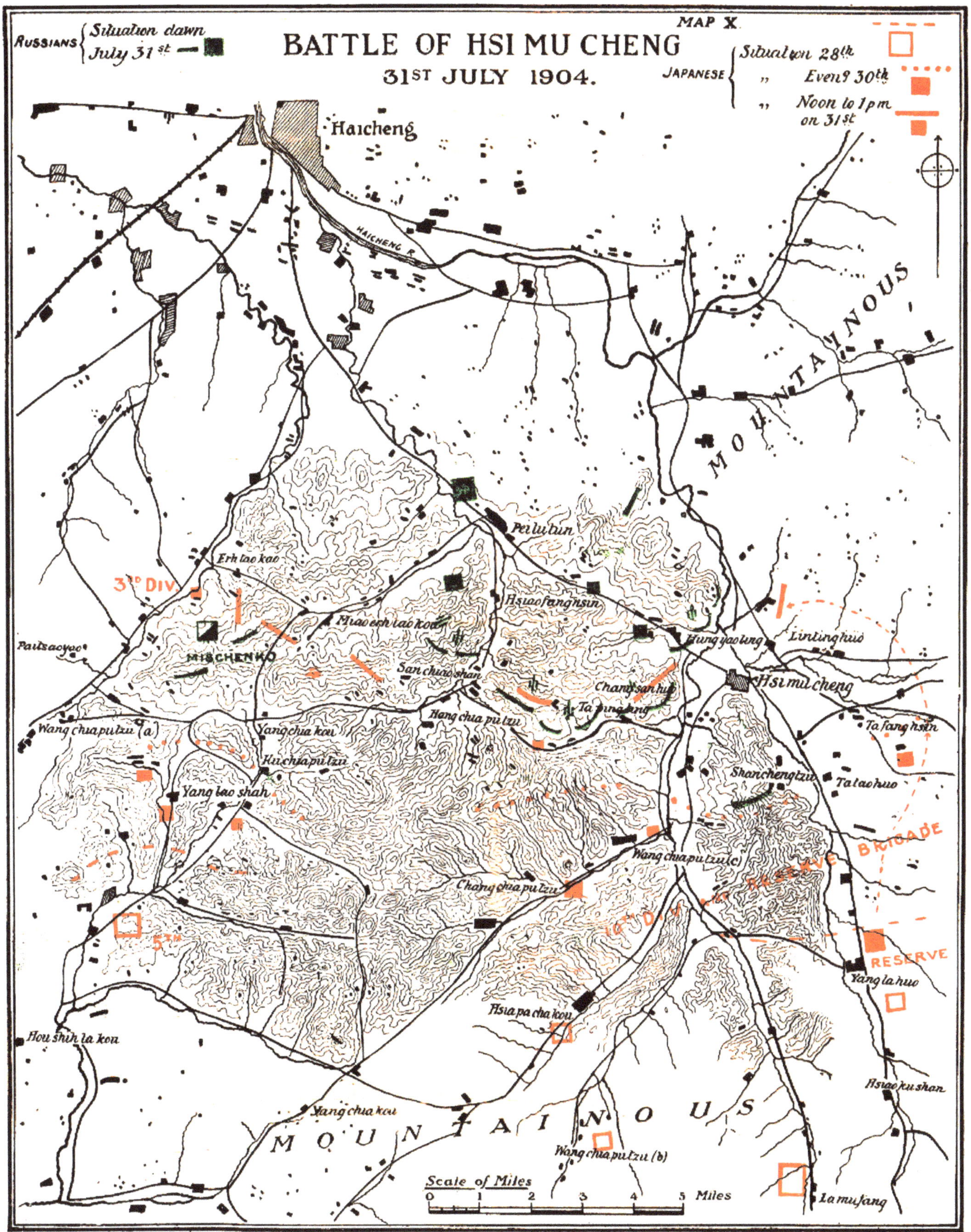

SWAN SONNENSCHEIN & Co. Ltd. LONDON

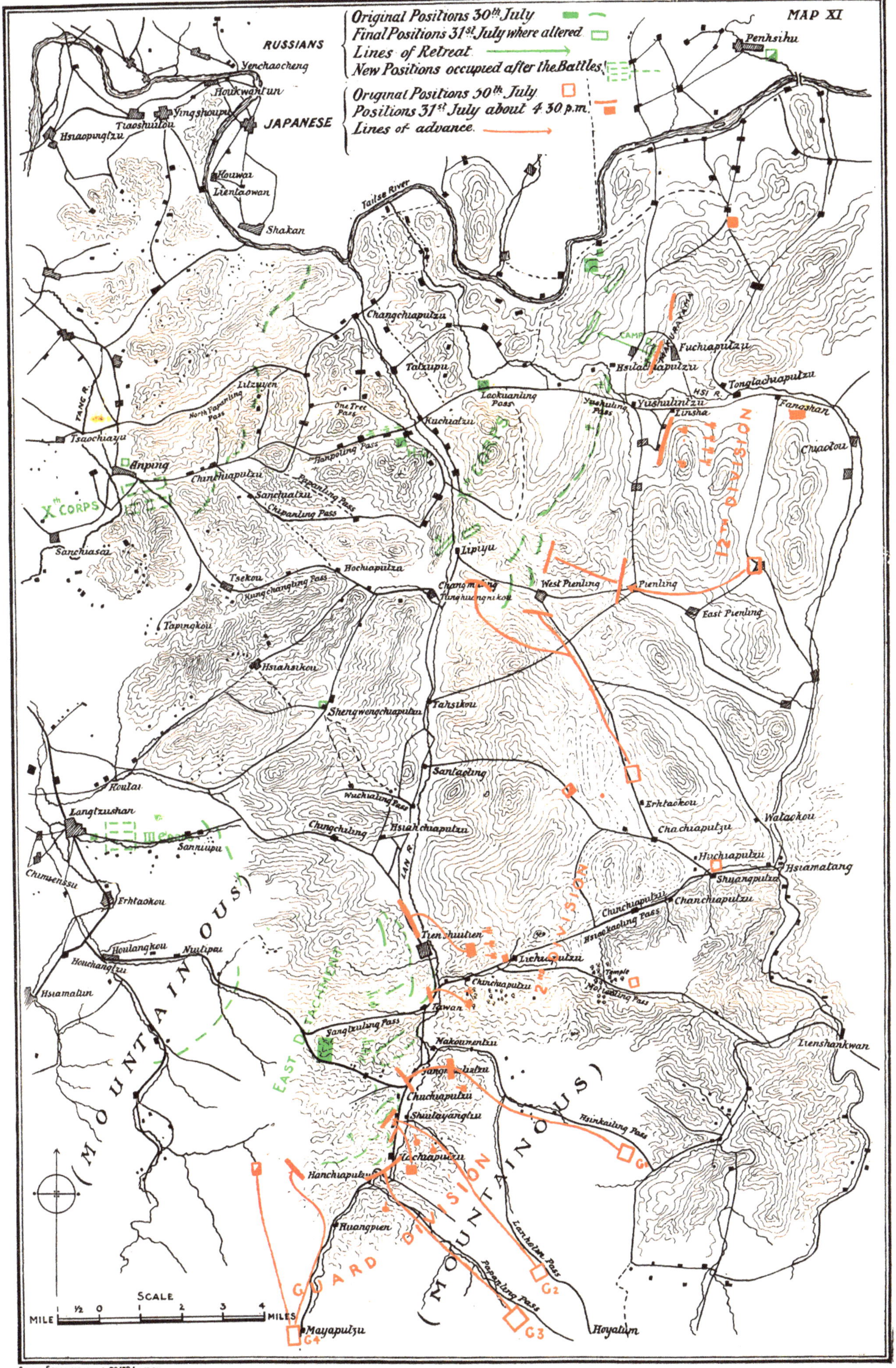

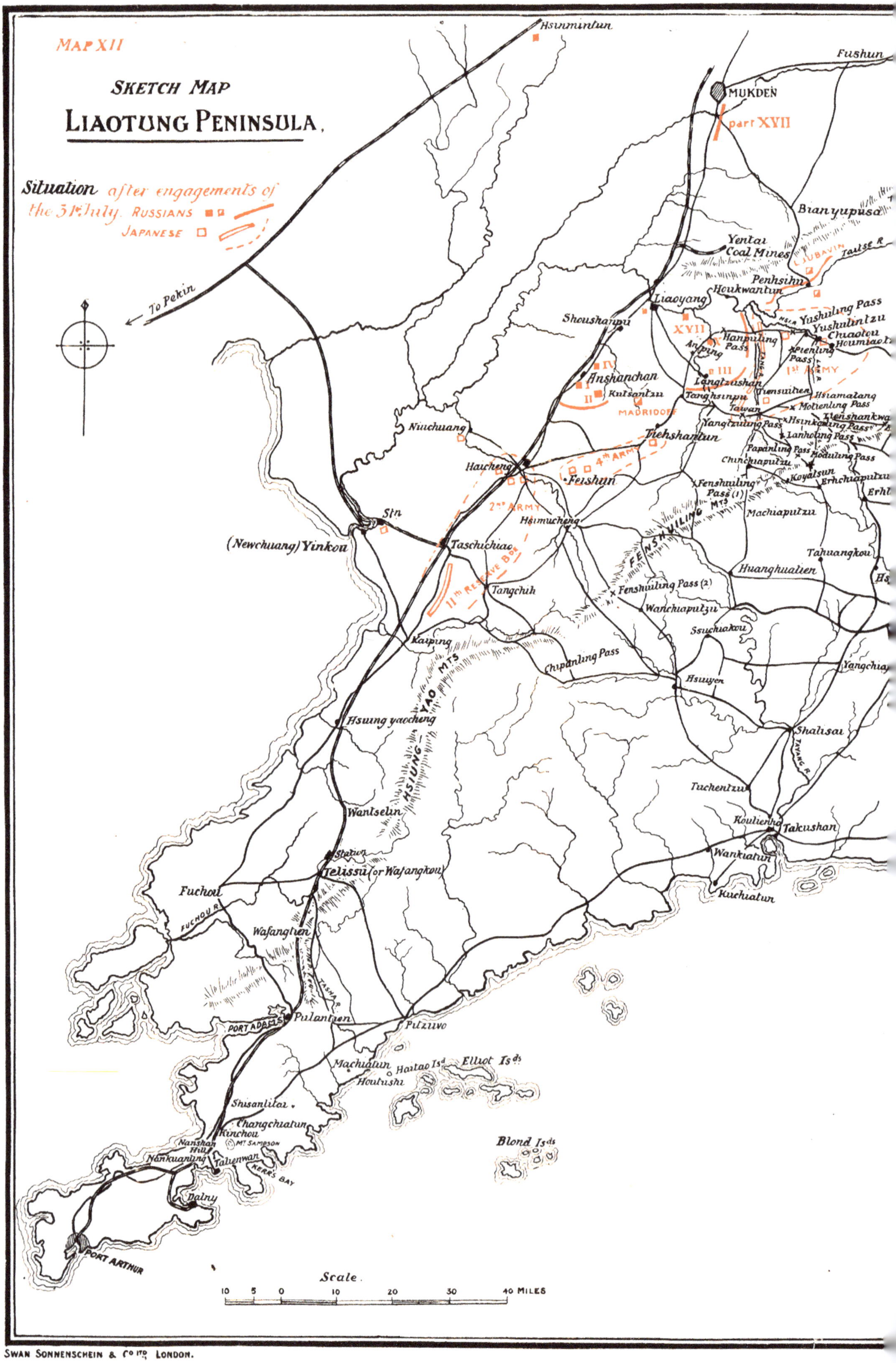

SWAN SONNENSCHEIN & Co Ltd. LONDON.

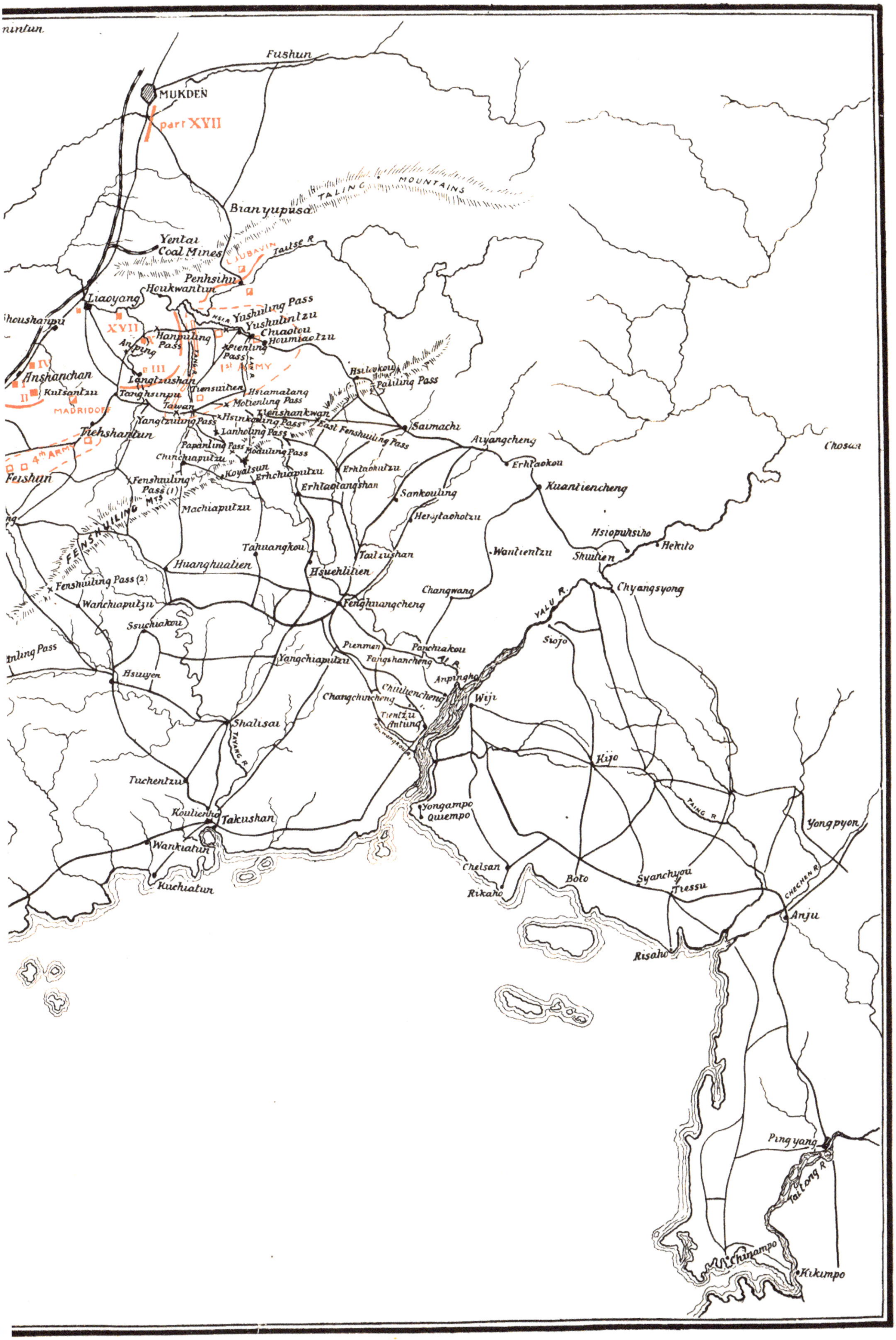

MUKDEN
Fushun
part XVII
TALING MOUNTAINS
Bianyupusa
Yentai Coal Mines
LJUBAVIN
Taitse R
Penhsihu
Liaoyang
Houkwantun
Yushuling Pass
Yushulintzu
Chiaotou
Houmiaotzu
XVII
Hanpuling Pass
Anping
Pienling Pass
1st ARMY
Anshanchan
Langtzushan
Hsilekou
Paliling Pass
Kutsantzu
Tanghsinpu
Tiensuitien
Hsiamatang
Motienling Pass
MADRIDOFF
Tawan
Tienshankwan
Yangtzuling Pass
Hsinkailing Pass
East Fenshuiling Pass
Saimachi
Tiehshantun
Lanhouling Pass
Papanling Pass
Moduling Pass
Aiyangcheng
4th ARMY
Chinchiaputzu
Koyalsun
Erhtaokutzu
Erhtaokou
Feishun
Fenshuiling Pass (1)
Erhchiaputzu
Erhtaotangshan
Kuantiencheng
Sankouling
Machiaputzu
FENSHUILING MTS
Hengtaohotzu
Hsiopuhsiho
Tahuangkou
Tailzushan
Wantientzu
Shuitien
Hekito
Huanghuatien
Hsuehlitien
Fenshuiling Pass (2)
Changwang
Chyangsyong
Wanchiaputzu
Fenghuangcheng
YALU R.
Ssuchiakou
Siojo
Pienmen
Panchiakou
Yangchiaputzu
Fangshancheng
Hsiuyen
Anpingho
Chiuliencheng
Wiji
Changchincheng
Tientzu
Antung
Shalisai
TAYANG R.
Kijo
Tuchentzu
Yongampo
Quiempo
TAING R
Koulientho
Takushan
Yongpyon
Wankiatun
Chelsan
Boto
Syanchyou
Tiessu
Rikaho
Kuchiatun
CHECHEN R.
Anju
Risaho
Chosun
Ping yang
Tai tong R
Chinampo
Kikimpo